CONNECTED MATHEMATICS

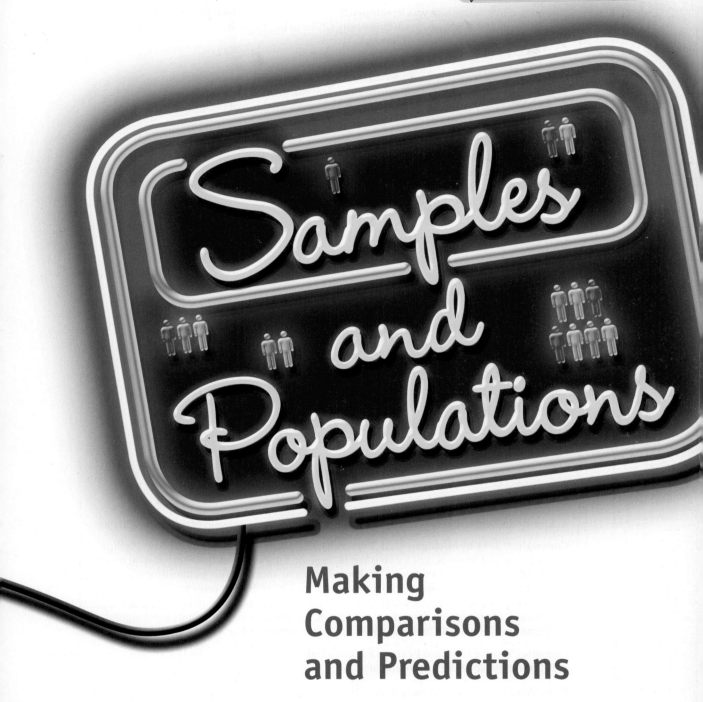

Samples and Populations

Making Comparisons and Predictions

Glenda Lappan, Elizabeth Difanis Phillips,
James T. Fey, Susan N. Friel

PEARSON

oston, Massachusetts • Chandler, Arizona • Glenview, Illinois • Upper Saddle River, New Jersey

Connected Mathematics® was developed at Michigan State University with financial support from the Michigan State University Office of the Provost, Computing and Technology, and the College of Natural Science.

This material is based upon work supported by the National Science Foundation under Grant No. MDR 9150217 and Grant No. ESI 9986372. Opinions expressed are those of the authors and not necessarily those of the Foundation.

As with prior editions of this work, the authors and administration of Michigan State University preserve a tradition of devoting royalties from this publication to support activities sponsored by the MSU Mathematics Education Enrichment Fund.

PEARSON

13-digit ISBN 978-0-13-327642-8
10-digit ISBN 0-13-327642-2
2 3 4 5 6 7 8 9 10 V011 17 16 15 14

A Team of Experts

Glenda Lappan is a University Distinguished Professor in the Program in Mathematics Education (PRIME) and the Department of Mathematics at Michigan State University. Her research and development interests are in the connected areas of students' learning of mathematics and mathematics teachers' professional growth and change related to the development and enactment of K–12 curriculum materials.

Elizabeth Difanis Phillips is a Senior Academic Specialist in the Program in Mathematics Education (PRIME) and the Department of Mathematics at Michigan State University. She is interested in teaching and learning mathematics for both teachers and students. These interests have led to curriculum and professional development projects at the middle school and high school levels, as well as projects related to the teaching and learning of algebra across the grades.

James T. Fey is a Professor Emeritus at the University of Maryland. His consistent professional interest has been development and research focused on curriculum materials that engage middle and high school students in problem-based collaborative investigations of mathematical ideas and their applications.

Susan N. Friel is a Professor of Mathematics Education in the School of Education at the University of North Carolina at Chapel Hill. Her research interests focus on statistics education for middle-grade students and, more broadly, on teachers' professional development and growth in teaching mathematics K–8.

With... Yvonne Grant and Jacqueline Stewart

Yvonne Grant teaches mathematics at Portland Middle School in Portland, Michigan. Jacqueline Stewart is a recently retired high school teacher of mathematics at Okemos High School in Okemos, Michigan. Both Yvonne and Jacqueline have worked on a variety of activities related to the development, implementation, and professional development of the CMP curriculum since its beginning in 1991.

Development Team

CMP3 Authors

Glenda Lappan, University Distinguished Professor, Michigan State University
Elizabeth Difanis Phillips, Senior Academic Specialist, Michigan State University
James T. Fey, Professor Emeritus, University of Maryland
Susan N. Friel, Professor, University of North Carolina – Chapel Hill

With...
Yvonne Grant, Portland Middle School, Michigan
Jacqueline Stewart, Mathematics Consultant, Mason, Michigan

In Memory of... William M. Fitzgerald, Professor (Deceased), Michigan State University, who made substantial contributions to conceptualizing and creating CMP1.

Administrative Assistant

Michigan State University
Judith Martus Miller

Support Staff

Michigan State University
Undergraduate Assistants:
Bradley Robert Corlett, Carly Fleming, Erin Lucian, Scooter Nowak

Development Assistants

Michigan State University
Graduate Research Assistants:
Richard "Abe" Edwards, Nic Gilbertson, Funda Gonulates, Aladar Horvath, Eun Mi Kim, Kevin Lawrence, Jennifer Nimtz, Joanne Philhower, Sasha Wang

Assessment Team

Maine
Falmouth Public Schools
Falmouth Middle School: Shawn Towle

Michigan
Ann Arbor Public Schools
Tappan Middle School
Anne Marie Nicoll-Turner

Portland Public Schools
Portland Middle School
Holly DeRosia, Yvonne Grant

Traverse City Area Public Schools
Traverse City East Middle School
Jane Porath, Mary Beth Schmitt

Traverse City West Middle School
Jennifer Rundio, Karrie Tufts

Ohio
Clark-Shawnee Local Schools
Rockway Middle School: Jim Mamer

Content Consultants

Michigan State University
Peter Lappan, Professor Emeritus, Department of Mathematics

Normandale Community College
Christopher Danielson, Instructor, Department of Mathematics & Statistics

University of North Carolina – Wilmington
Dargan Frierson, Jr., Professor, Department of Mathematics & Statistics

Student Activities
Michigan State University
Brin Keller, Associate Professor, Department of Mathematics

Consultants

Indiana
Purdue University
Mary Bouck, Mathematics Consultant

Michigan
Oakland Schools
Valerie Mills, Mathematics Education Supervisor
Mathematics Education Consultants:
Geraldine Devine, Dana Gosen

Ellen Bacon, Independent Mathematics Consultant

New York
University of Rochester
Jeffrey Choppin, Associate Professor

Ohio
University of Toledo
Debra Johanning, Associate Professor

Pennsylvania
University of Pittsburgh
Margaret Smith, Professor

Texas
University of Texas at Austin
Emma Trevino, Supervisor of Mathematics Programs, The Dana Center

Mathematics for All Consulting
Carmen Whitman, Mathematics Consultant

....

Reviewers

Michigan
Ionia Public Schools
Kathy Dole, Director of Curriculum and Instruction

Grand Valley State University
Lisa Kasmer, Assistant Professor

Portland Public Schools
Teri Keusch, Classroom Teacher

Minnesota
Hopkins School District 270
Michele Luke, Mathematics Coordinator

....

Field Test Sites for CMP3

Michigan
Ann Arbor Public Schools
Tappan Middle School
Anne Marie Nicoll-Turner*

Portland Public Schools
Portland Middle School: Mark Braun, Angela Buckland, Holly DeRosia, Holly Feldpausch, Angela Foote, Yvonne Grant*, Kristin Roberts, Angie Stump, Tammi Wardwell

Traverse City Area Public Schools
Traverse City East Middle School
Ivanka Baic Berkshire, Brenda Dunscombe, Tracie Herzberg, Deb Larimer, Jan Palkowski, Rebecca Perreault, Jane Porath*, Robert Sagan, Mary Beth Schmitt*

Traverse City West Middle School
Pamela Alfieri, Jennifer Rundio, Maria Taplin, Karrie Tufts*

Maine
Falmouth Public Schools
Falmouth Middle School: Sally Bennett, Chris Driscoll, Sara Jones, Shawn Towle*

Minnesota
Minneapolis Public Schools
Jefferson Community School
Leif Carlson*,
Katrina Hayek Munsisoumang*

Ohio
Clark-Shawnee Local Schools
Reid School: Joanne Gilley
Rockway Middle School: Jim Mamer*
Possum School: Tami Thomas

*Indicates a Field Test Site Coordinator

Samples and Populations

Making Comparisons and Predictions

3

Using Samples to Draw Conclusions   56

Looking Ahead

How can you determine whether steel-frame roller coasters or wood-frame roller coasters are faster?

A national magazine posts a survey on its Web site for its readers. **What** population do the survey results describe? Is sampling with this kind of plan a good way to draw conclusions about an entire population?

We need student volunteers for our survey.

How can you estimate the albatross population of an island?

The United States Census attempts to gather information from every household in the United States. Gathering, organizing, and analyzing data from such a large population is expensive and time-consuming. In most studies of large populations, data are gathered from a *sample* of the population.

Sampling is an important tool in statistics and data analysis. You can draw conclusions about a single population or compare samples from different populations. For example, scientists may study a sample of penguins to learn more about the entire population of penguins.

Recall that you can analyze a set of data by finding summary statistics. You can use measures of center and measures of variability to describe a distribution.

In this Unit, you will learn how to choose a sample of data from a large population and use data distributions and statistics to draw conclusions about that population. You will use these ideas to answer questions such as those on the previous page.

Making Comparisons and Predictions

In *Samples and Populations*, you will learn about different ways to collect and analyze data in order to make comparisons and draw conclusions.

You will learn how to:

- Use the process of statistical investigation to answer questions

- Apply concepts from probability to select random samples from populations

- Gather information about a population by examining a sample of the population

- Use information from samples to draw conclusions about populations

- Identify how sample sizes and sampling plans influence the measures of center and variability that describe a sample distribution

- Compare samples using measures of center (mean, median), measures of variability (range, IQR, MAD), and displays that group data (histograms, box-and-whisker plots)

When you encounter a new problem, it is a good idea to ask yourself questions. In this Unit, you might ask questions such as:

What is the population?

What is the sample?

Is the sample a representative sample?

How can I describe the data I collected?

How can I use my results to draw conclusions about the population?

How can I use samples to compare two or more populations?

Mathematical Practices and Habits of Mind

In the *Connected Mathematics* curriculum you will develop an understanding of important mathematical ideas by solving problems and reflecting on the mathematics involved. Every day, you will use "habits of mind" to make sense of problems and apply what you learn to new situations. Some of these habits are described by the *Common Core State Standards for Mathematical Practices* (MP).

MP1 Make sense of problems and persevere in solving them.

When using mathematics to solve a problem, it helps to think carefully about

- data and other facts you are given and what additional information you need to solve the problem;
- strategies you have used to solve similar problems and whether you could solve a related simpler problem first;
- how you could express the problem with equations, diagrams, or graphs;
- whether your answer makes sense.

MP2 Reason abstractly and quantitatively.

When you are asked to solve a problem, it often helps to

- focus first on the key mathematical ideas;
- check that your answer makes sense in the problem setting;
- use what you know about the problem setting to guide your mathematical reasoning.

MP3 Construct viable arguments and critique the reasoning of others.

When you are asked to explain why a conjecture is correct, you can

- show some examples that fit the claim and explain why they fit;
- show how a new result follows logically from known facts and principles.

When you believe a mathematical claim is incorrect, you can

- show one or more counterexamples—cases that don't fit the claim;
- find steps in the argument that do not follow logically from prior claims.

MP4 Model with mathematics.

When you are asked to solve problems, it often helps to

- think carefully about the numbers or geometric shapes that are the most important factors in the problem, then ask yourself how those factors are related to each other;
- express data and relationships in the problem with tables, graphs, diagrams, or equations, and check your result to see if it makes sense.

MP5 Use appropriate tools strategically.

When working on mathematical questions, you should always

- decide which tools are most helpful for solving the problem and why;
- try a different tool when you get stuck.

MP6 Attend to precision.

In every mathematical exploration or problem-solving task, it is important to

- think carefully about the required accuracy of results; is a number estimate or geometric sketch good enough, or is a precise value or drawing needed?
- report your discoveries with clear and correct mathematical language that can be understood by those to whom you are speaking or writing.

MP7 Look for and make use of structure.

In mathematical explorations and problem solving, it is often helpful to

- look for patterns that show how data points, numbers, or geometric shapes are related to each other;
- use patterns to make predictions.

MP8 Look for and express regularity in repeated reasoning.

When results of a repeated calculation show a pattern, it helps to

- express that pattern as a general rule that can be used in similar cases;
- look for shortcuts that will make the calculation simpler in other cases.

You will use all of the Mathematical Practices in this Unit. Sometimes, when you look at a Problem, it is obvious which practice is most helpful. At other times, you will decide on a practice to use during class explorations and discussions. After completing each Problem, ask yourself:

- What mathematics have I learned by solving this Problem?
- What Mathematical Practices were helpful in learning this mathematics?

Making Sense of Samples

People often want to know what is typical in a given situation. For example, you might want to find out your typical math test score. You may investigate the typical number of text messages sent by students in a middle-school class. You can gather information to determine the typical batting average of a baseball player. You can collect and examine data to analyze situations such as these.

All data sets include some *variability*. Not all math scores are the same. Not all students send the same number of texts. Not all baseball players perform the same at bat. Statistical investigations pose questions with variable outcomes.

Common Core State Standards

7.SP.B.4 Use measures of center and measures of variability for numerical data from random samples to draw informal comparative inferences about two populations.

Essential for 7.SP.B.3 Informally assess the degree of visual overlap of two numerical data distributions with similar variabilities, measuring the difference between the centers by expressing it as a multiple of a measure of variability.

Also 7.NS.A.1 and 7.NS.A.1b, essential for 7.SP.A.1 and 7.SP.A.2

1.1 Comparing Performances
Using Center and Spread

 The spreadsheet below shows the math test scores earned by two students, Jun and Mia, in the first quarter of 7th grade.

File	Edit	Tool	View	Chart	Class	Help

| | | | | **Math Test Scores** | | | | **Math Homework** | |

Class	Name	Student Number	Test 1	Test 2	Test 3	Test 4	Test 5	Test 6	Test Average
001	Jun	09	80	60	100				
001	Mia	22	75	80	85				

The math test scores are *samples* of the math test scores for each student throughout the school year. You can use data from samples to make general statements about overall performance.

- Who performs better on math tests, Jun or Mia? Explain.

In Problem 1.1, you will use measures of center and measures of variability, or spread, to determine who performs more consistently on tests.

Problem 1.1

A 1. Find the *mean* and *median* of Jun's scores. What do you notice?

2. Find the mean and median of Mia's scores. What do you notice?

3. Use the measures of center you found in parts (1) and (2). Compare Jun's and Mia's test performances.

Problem 1.1 *continued*

B　**1.** Determine the *range* and *mean absolute deviation (MAD)* of Jun's test scores.

　　2. Determine the range and MAD of Mia's test scores.

　　3. Use the measures of spread you found in parts (1) and (2). Compare Jun's and Mia's test performances.

C　Do you have enough data to make any general statements about Jun's or Mia's overall math test performance? Explain.

D　The spreadsheet below shows Jun's and Mia's test scores at mid-year.

File　Edit　Tool　View　Chart　Class　Help								
Math Test Scores				**Math Homework**				
Class	**Name**	**Student Number**	**Test 1**	**Test 2**	**Test 3**	**Test 4**	**Test 5**	**Test 6**	**Test Average**
001	Jun	09	80	60	100	80	80	80	
001	Mia	22	75	80	85	80	80	100	

　1. Find the median and mean of Jun's test data and of Mia's test data. Use each measure of center to compare Jun's scores and Mia's scores.

　2. Find the range and MAD of Jun's test data and of Mia's test data. Use each measure of variability to compare Jun's scores and Mia's scores.

　3. Decide whether you agree or disagree with each statement below. Use the statistics you found in parts (1) and (2). Explain your reasoning.

- One student is a stronger math student than the other.

- One student is more consistent than the other.

- The two students perform equally well on math tests.

- You can make better comparisons using the larger data set.

ACE Homework starts on page 20.

1.2 Which Team Is Most Successful?
Using the MAD to Compare Samples

A middle school's Hiking Club holds a fundraiser each spring. The club sells granola bars and packages of trail mix. The 35 club members form six fundraising teams. Each team is a *sample* of students from the club. The most successful team receives a prize.

The faculty advisor posts the money the teams raised on a bulletin board.

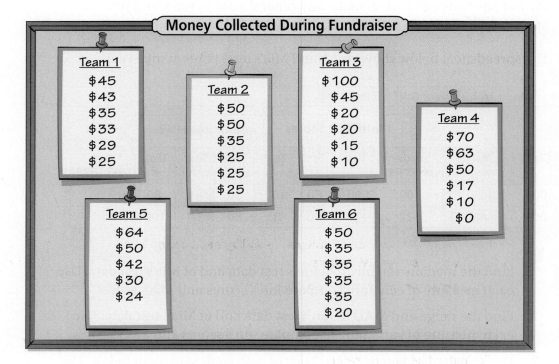

- Which team is the most successful and deserves to win the prize? Explain.

Problem 1.2

A Make a *line plot* of each team's data. Use a scale that makes it easy to compare results among teams. Write three sentences that compare the *distributions*.

B The Hiking Club's organizers must decide which team is awarded the prize. Each organizer has a different strategy for determining the most successful fundraising team.

For each strategy below, explain whether or not the strategy helps determine the most successful team. If the strategy helps determine the most successful team, determine who will win the prize.

1. **Bianca**

For each team, just add up all the money raised by its members. Then compare the team totals.

2. **Gianna**

Find the mean number of dollars raised by each team. Then compare the team averages.

3. **Jonah**

Compare the money raised by each member to the team's average. On average, how far does each member's amount differ from the team's mean amount? For each team, find the MAD. Then compare the MADs of the six teams.

C What other strategies might you use? How does your strategy help you determine which team was most successful?

continued on the next page >

Problem **1.2** *continued*

D In Question A, you made line plots of the six sets of data. In Question B, part (3), you found the mean absolute deviation (MAD) of each of the six distributions.

The dot plot below shows Team 1's fundraising amounts. The red lines indicate the distances of one MAD and two MADs from the mean on either side. Count the data points located closer than, but not including, the distance of one MAD from the mean. (The △ indicates the mean, 35.)

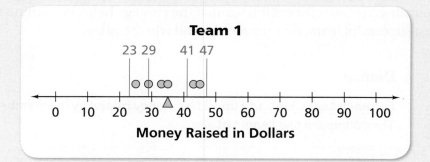

1. How many of Team 1's data values are located *within one MAD* (both less than and greater than the mean)? Write this number as a percent.

2. How many of Team 1's data values are located *within two MADs* of the mean? Write this number as a percent.

3. How many of Team 1's data values are located *more than two MADs* away from the mean? Write this number as a percent.

4. Repeat parts (1)–(3) for each of the other teams' data. For each team, use the team's MAD to analyze the distribution.

5. Use the MAD locations from parts (1)–(4) to describe how each team's data values spread around the mean of the data.

Ⓐ Ⓒ Ⓔ Homework starts on page 20.

1.3 Pick Your Preference
Distinguishing Categorical Data From Numerical Data

In this Unit, you have worked with *numerical data,* which are counts or measures. Sometimes, however, the answers to survey questions can be sorted into categories or groups, such as your birth month, favorite movie, or eye color. These answers are *categorical data.* You can count categorical data, but you cannot place them in numerical order.

A survey about roller coasters asks these questions:

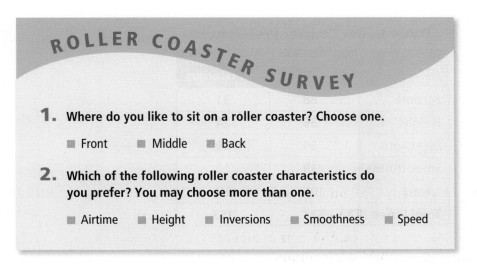

ROLLER COASTER SURVEY

1. **Where do you like to sit on a roller coaster? Choose one.**

   ■ Front ■ Middle ■ Back

2. **Which of the following roller coaster characteristics do you prefer? You may choose more than one.**

   ■ Airtime ■ Height ■ Inversions ■ Smoothness ■ Speed

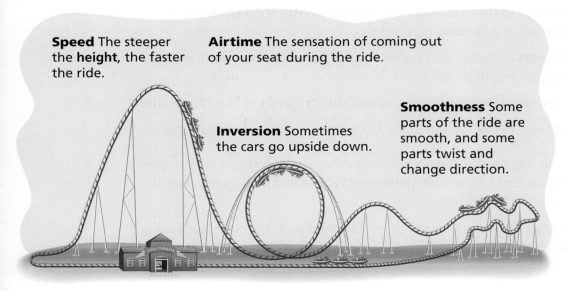

Speed The steeper the **height**, the faster the ride.

Airtime The sensation of coming out of your seat during the ride.

Inversion Sometimes the cars go upside down.

Smoothness Some parts of the ride are smooth, and some parts twist and change direction.

The tables below show the Roller Coaster Survey responses collected from Internet respondents and from a group of 7th-grade students.

Roller Coaster Seating Preferences

Preference	Votes From Internet	Votes From 7th Graders
Front	97	27
Middle	50	22
Back	18	14
Total Votes	**165**	**63**

Other Roller Coaster Preferences

Preference	Votes From Internet	Votes From 7th Graders
Airtime	88	31
Height	36	24
Inversions	59	29
Smoothness	39	12
Speed	105	57
Total Votes	**327**	**153**

Notice the four different *samples* reported:

- Answers to the first Roller Coaster Survey question from Internet respondents

- Answers to the second Roller Coaster Survey question from Internet respondents

- Answers to the first Roller Coaster Survey question from 7th graders

- Answers to the second Roller Coaster Survey question from 7th graders

The table shows that 165 people responded to the Internet survey about seating. Of those, 97 people prefer to sit at the front. The *frequency* of the response "front" is 97.

- What is the frequency of 7th graders who prefer to sit at the front of a roller coaster?

Suppose you want to find out which group includes more people who prefer to sit at the front.

The sample sizes of Internet respondents and 7th graders are different. You can use **relative frequencies**—frequencies based on percentages—to compare samples of different sizes. For example, $\frac{97}{165} \approx 0.59$, so about 59% of the people who voted online prefer to sit at the front of a roller coaster.

Relative Frequency

$\frac{97}{165} \approx 59\%$

Survey Responses

	Internet	7th Graders
Prefers Front	97	27
Total	165	63

- How can you compare the results of a survey to see whether each group responded to the questions in a similar way?

Problem 1.3

A As a class, answer the two Roller Coaster Survey questions. On a copy of the tables on the previous page, record your class data.

B For each survey question, make *bar graphs* of the three data sets: the Internet data, the 7th-grade data, and your class data. Use percents to report relative frequencies on your bar graphs.

C Which measure(s) of center—*mean, median,* or *mode*—can you use to describe these results? Explain.

D 1. For each survey question, write two statements comparing results from the three data sets.

    2. Write two statements to summarize the data collected from the Roller Coaster Survey. How are the summaries useful?

E Suppose 400 people ride a roller coaster in one day. How many of them would you predict want to sit at the front? Explain.

A C E Homework starts on page 20.

1.4 Are Steel-Frame Coasters Faster Than Wood-Frame Coasters?
Using the IQR to Compare Samples

Have you ever wondered how many roller coasters there are in the world? The table below displays data from a **census.** It shows information about the **population**, or entire collection, of roller coasters worldwide. About 95% of the coasters are steel-frame coasters; about 5% are wood-frame coasters.

Roller Coaster Census

Roller Coaster Count				Some Types of Steel-Frame Coasters			
Continent	Total	Wood	Steel	Inverted	Stand Up	Suspended	Sit Down
Africa	59	0	59	3	0	0	56
Asia	1,455	13	1,442	47	4	16	1,362
Australia	24	3	21	2	0	0	19
Europe	822	35	787	28	1	12	733
North America	764	122	642	50	10	5	561
South America	142	1	141	3	0	4	134
Total	3,266	174	3,092	133	15	37	2,865

SOURCE: *Roller Coaster DataBase*

- How do you think the roller-coaster census data were collected?

In this Problem, you will use data from a sample of 30 steel-frame roller coasters and data from a sample of 30 wood-frame roller coasters. The table below shows some data from the samples.

Roller-Coaster Sample Data

Steel-Frame Roller Coasters	Top Speed (mi/h)	Duration (min)
Steel-Frame Coaster A	22	1.50
Steel-Frame Coaster B	40	1.53
Steel-Frame Coaster C	50	2.00
Steel-Frame Coaster D	70	0.55
Wood-Frame Roller Coasters	Top Speed (mi/h)	Duration (min)
Wood-Frame Coaster A	50	1.75
Wood-Frame Coaster B	50	1.83
Wood-Frame Coaster C	55	2.00
Wood-Frame Coaster D	62	2.50

 How might you decide which are faster, steel-frame roller coasters or wood-frame roller coasters? Explain.

 Problem 1.4

Use the samples of roller-coaster data provided by your teacher for Questions A–D.

Ⓐ 1. What do you consider to be a fast speed for a roller coaster? Explain.

    2. Suppose you want to ride the faster of two roller coasters. Does knowing each roller coaster's top speed help you make the decision? Explain.

    3. Do you think steel-frame roller coasters are faster than wood-frame roller coasters? Use the top-speed data to justify your answer.

continued on the next page >

Problem 1.4 *continued*

B The dot plots below show the top-speed data from the sample of 30 steel-frame coasters and 30 wood-frame coasters. The mean is marked with a blue triangle (△). Use the dot plots to answer parts (1)–(3).

Steel-Frame Roller Coaster Speeds

Mean = 55.03 mi/h
MAD = 14.64 mi/h

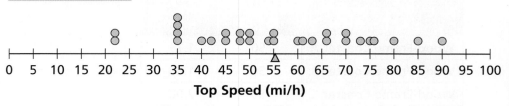

Top Speed (mi/h)

Wood-Frame Roller Coaster Speeds

Mean = 52.6 mi/h
MAD = 7.47 mi/h

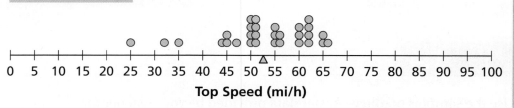

Top Speed (mi/h)

1. Identify the minimum and maximum values, ranges, and means of each distribution. Use these statistics to compare the speeds of steel-frame and wood-frame roller coasters.

2. Identify the median and the *interquartile range (IQR)* of each distribution. Use the medians and IQRs to compare the speeds of steel-frame and wood-frame roller coasters.

3. Make a *box-and-whisker plot*, or box plot, of each distribution. Use the same scale for each graph. Use the box plots to compare the speeds of steel-frame and wood-frame roller coasters.

Problem 1.4 continued

C Compare your answer to Question A, part (3) with your answers to Question B. Are steel-frame roller coasters faster than wood-frame roller coasters? Explain your reasoning.

D Charlie and Rosa wrote the reports below. They used the two distributions of data to compare steel-frame roller coasters and wood-frame roller coasters. Do you agree with Charlie or with Rosa? Explain your reasoning.

Charlie

I found that the means and medians are about the same for each distribution. If I looked at the box plots and the statistics, I would say that steel-frame roller coasters are slightly faster than wood-frame roller coasters.

When I made the box plots, I noticed that the data distribution for wood-frame roller coasters has two outliers. I know that low or high data values shift the mean. In this case, the outliers made the mean speed of the wood-frame roller coasters shift down below the median.

So keeping the outliers in mind, I concluded that steel-frame roller coasters and wood-frame roller coasters have similar speeds.

Rosa

The measures of center were all pretty close, so i looked at the measures of spread. The IQR helped me see that there is greater variability in the steel-frame roller coasters than in the wood-frame roller coasters.

I looked at the top 25% of all roller-coaster speeds. The top speeds for wood-frame roller coasters are around 60–66 mi/h and steel-frame roller coasters have top speeds around 70–90 mi/h.

Steel-frame roller coasters have faster speeds than wood-frame roller coasters, but not all steel-frame roller coasters are faster than all wood-frame roller coasters.

 Homework starts on page 20.

Applications

For all Exercises, use your calculator when needed.

For Exercises 1 and 2, use the table below.

Diving Scores

Diver	Dive 1	Dive 2	Dive 3	Dive 4	Dive 5
Jarrod	8.5	8.1	6.4	9.5	10.0
Pascal	9.3	7.5	8.0	8.5	9.2

1. **a.** Find the mean and the median of Jarrod's diving scores. Compare the mean and the median.

   b. Find the mean and the median of Pascal's diving scores. Compare the mean and the median.

   c. Use measures of center to compare Jarrod's and Pascal's diving results. What can you say about their performances?

2. **a.** Find the range and the MAD of Jarrod's scores.

   b. Find the range and the MAD of Pascal's scores.

   c. Use measures of spread to compare Jarrod's and Pascal's diving results. What can you say about their performances?

The Soccer Club holds a flavored-popcorn fundraiser each fall. The 23 club members form four teams. The most successful team receives a prize. For Exercises 3–7, use the data in the table below.

Money Collected During Fundraiser (dollars)

Team 1	Team 2	Team 3	Team 4
55	56	100	80
53	53	50	73
44	50	40	44
44	38	40	38
39	37	25	35
35	36	15	

3. Find the total amount of money collected by each team. Do the totals help you determine the most successful team? Explain.

4. **a.** What is the mean amount of money collected by each team? The median?

   b. Do either of these measures of center help you determine the most successful team? Explain.

5. **a.** For each team, find the range and MAD.

   b. Do either of these measures of spread help you determine the most successful team? Explain.

For Exercises 6 and 7, use the table above. Answer each question for Teams 1–4.

6. **a.** How many of the team's data values are located *within one MAD* of the mean (both less than and greater than the mean)? Write this number as a percent.

   b. How many of the team's data values are located *within two MADs* of the mean? Write this number as a percent.

   c. How many of the team's data values are located *more than two MADs* away from the mean? Write this number as a percent.

7. Use your calculations from Exercise 6. Does any team have a member who raised much more (or much less) money than the other team members? Explain your reasoning.

8. The following question was asked in a survey:

What is your favorite amusement-park ride?

■ Roller Coaster   ■ Log Ride   ■ Ferris Wheel   ■ Bumper Cars

The tablet below shows the results from an Internet survey and from surveys of 7th-grade students at East Jr. High and West Jr. High.

Favorite Amusement Park Rides

Favorite Ride	Votes From the Internet	Votes From East Jr. High	Votes From West Jr. High
Roller Coaster	92	42	36
Log Ride	26	31	14
Ferris Wheel	22	3	6
Bumper Cars	20	4	4
Total Votes	160	80	60

a. Make bar graphs for each of the three data sets: the Internet survey data, the data from East Jr. High, and the data from West Jr. High. Use percents to show relative frequencies.

b. Write three or more statements comparing the data sets.

For Exercises 9–13, use the Roller Coaster Census from Problem 1.4 to complete the statements below.

9. For every one wood-frame roller coaster there are about ■ steel-frame roller coasters.

10. North America has about ■ times as many roller coasters as South America.

11. Asia has about ■ times as many roller coasters as North America.

12. North America has ▦ % of all the wood-frame roller coasters in the world.

13. Write two of your own comparison statements.

14. Use the dot plots below. For each part (a)–(c), answer the questions for each distribution.

Steel-Frame Roller Coaster Speeds

Mean = 55.03 mi/h
MAD = 14.64 mi/h

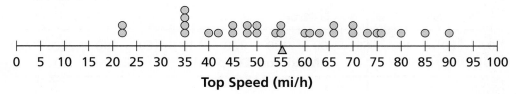

Top Speed (mi/h)

Wood-Frame Roller Coaster Speeds

Mean = 52.6 mi/h
MAD = 7.47 mi/h

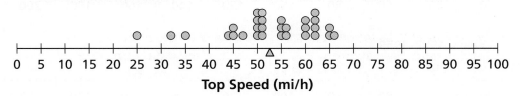

Top Speed (mi/h)

a. How many roller coasters have speeds within one MAD of the mean (both less than and greater than the mean)? Write this number as a percent.

b. How many roller coasters have speeds within two MADs of the mean? Write this number as a percent.

c. How many roller coasters have speeds more than two MADs away from the mean? Write this number as a percent.

15. The three pairs of dot plots below show data for 50 wood-frame roller coasters. Each mean is marked with a △ . Each median is marked with a ⊥. Use the dot plots to answer the questions on the next page.

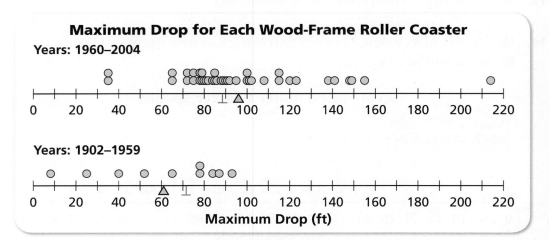

Maximum Drop for Each Wood-Frame Roller Coaster

Years: 1960–2004

Years: 1902–1959

Maximum Drop (ft)

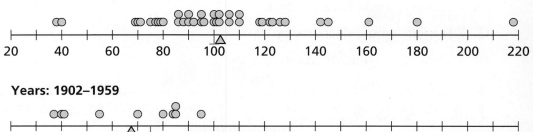

Maximum Height for Each Wood-Frame Roller Coaster

Years: 1960–2004

Years: 1902–1959

Maximum Height (ft)

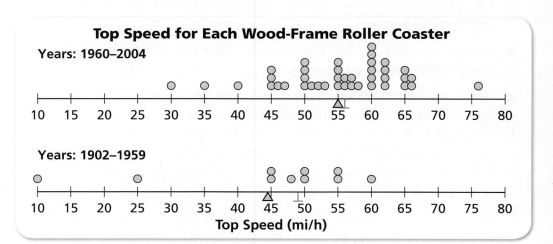

Top Speed for Each Wood-Frame Roller Coaster

Years: 1960–2004

Years: 1902–1959

Top Speed (mi/h)

a. Write three statements comparing wood-frame roller coasters built before 1960 with wood-frame roller coasters built in 1960 or later.

b. Hector said there are too few roller coasters to make comparisons. Do you agree with Hector? Explain.

16. **Multiple Choice** Most of the data values in a distribution will be located—

   A. more than two MADs away from the mean.

   B. within two MADs of the mean.

   C. within one MAD of the mean.

Connections

17. **Multiple Choice** Suppose the data value 27 is added to the set of data 10, 29, 15, 29, 35, and 2. Which statement is true?

   F. The mean would increase by 4.

   G. The mode would decrease by 10.

   H. The median would decrease by 1.

   J. None of the above.

18. **Multiple Choice** The mean of six numbers is 25. If one of the numbers is 15, what is the mean of the other five numbers?

   A. 15   B. 25   C. 27   D. 40

19. **Multiple Choice** Jasper's test scores for eight exams are below.

   $$84, 72, 88, 84, 92, 94, 78, \text{ and } x$$

   If the median of his scores is 86, what is a possible value for x?

   F. 68   G. 84   H. 86   J. 95

20. **Multiple Choice** In Mr. Ramirez's math class, there are three times as many girls as boys. The girls' mean grade on a recent quiz was 90. The boys' mean grade was 86. What was the mean grade for the class altogether?

   A. 88   B. 44   C. 89   D. 95

21. The tables below show the results of a survey of children ages 5 to 15. Use the data to answer the questions on the next page.

Table 1: Years Lived in Current Home

Years	Children	Percent
<1	639	7.9%
1	776	9.6%
2	733	9.0%
3	735	▪
4	587	7.2%
5	612	7.5%
6	487	6.0%
7	431	5.3%
8	442	5.4%
9	412	5.1%
10	492	6.0%
11	520	6.5%
12	508	6.3%
13	339	4.1%
14	225	2.8%
15	176	2.2%
Total	8,114	100%

SOURCE: *National Geographic*

Table 2: Apartments or Houses Lived in Since Birth

Number of Apartments or Houses	Children	Percent
1	1,645	20.7%
2	1,957	24.7%
3	1,331	16.8%
4	968	▪
5	661	8.3%
6	487	6.1%
7	291	3.7%
8	184	2.3%
9	80	1.0%
10	330	4.2%
Total	7,934	100%

Table 3: Cities or Towns Lived in Since Birth

Number of Cities or Towns	Boys	Girls	Ages 5–12	Ages 13–15
1	▪	42.2%	42.1%	40.9%
>1	58.9%	57.8%	▪	59.1%
Total	100%	100%	100%	100%

a. Find the missing percents in each table. Explain how you found them.

b. Make a bar graph to display the information in the third column of Table 2.

c. Write a summary paragraph about Table 2.

d. What percent of children have lived in the same home for 10 or more years? Justify your answer.

e. What percent of children have lived in only one home since they were born? Justify your answer.

f. About what fraction of the boys have lived in the same city or town all their lives? Explain.

22. The titles of the two circle graphs below are not shown. Use the data from the Roller Coaster Census in Problem 1.4. Which title goes with which graph? Explain.

Title 1: Wood-Frame Roller Coasters by Continent

Title 2: Steel-Frame Roller Coasters by Continent

a.

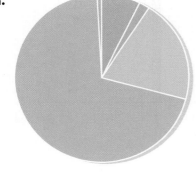

b.

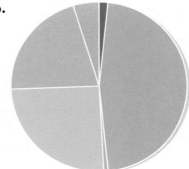

Key: ■ Africa   ▨ Europe
        ▨ Asia   ▨ North America
        ▨ Australia   ▨ South America

For Exercises 23 and 24, use the dot plot below. The dot plot shows the
amount of sugar per serving in 47 cereals.

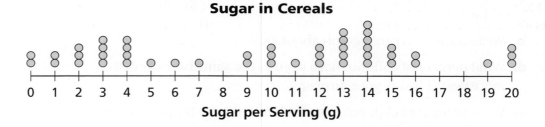

Sugar in Cereals

Sugar per Serving (g)

23. Describe the shape of the distribution above.

24. Estimate the locations of the mean and the median. How does the
shape of the distribution influence your estimates?

For Exercises 25 and 26, use the dot plot below. The dot plot shows the
serving sizes of 47 cereals.

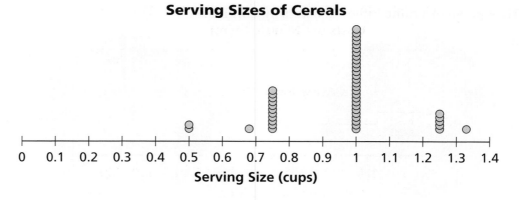

Serving Sizes of Cereals

Serving Size (cups)

25. Describe the distribution of serving sizes.

26. Estimate the locations of the mean and the median. How does the
shape of the distribution influence your estimates?

Extensions

For Exercises 27–32, use the dot plots and box plots below. The dot plots show the resting and exercise heart rates for a 7th-grade class.

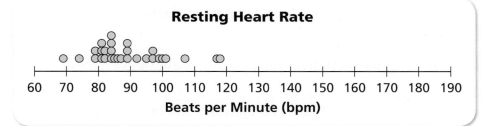

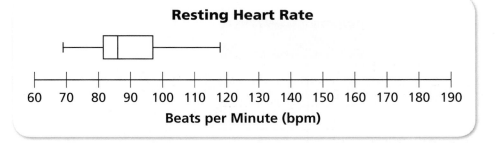

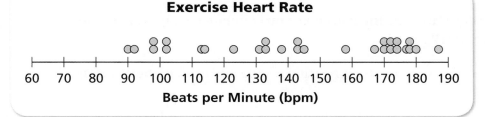

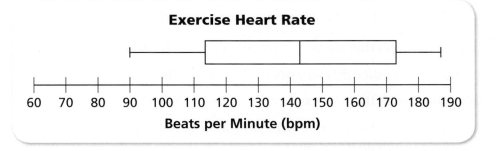

For Exercises 27–32, use the dot plots and box plots on the previous page.

27. Suppose you were given two means: 143.3 bpm and 89.4 bpm. Which mean is for the distribution of resting heart rates? Exercise heart rates? Explain.

28. Suppose you were given two MADs: 27.3 bpm and 8.9 bpm. Which MAD is for the distribution of resting heart rates? Exercise heart rates? Explain.

29. How does knowing the MADs help you compare resting and exercise heart rates?

30. Suppose you were given two IQRs: 15.5 bpm and 59.5 bpm. Which IQR is for the distribution of resting heart rates? Exercise heart rates? Explain.

31. How does knowing the IQRs help you compare resting and exercise heart rates?

32. Write three statements comparing resting and exercise heart rates.

33. The frequency table below shows the numbers of students who earned each grade in a teacher's math classes.

Letter Grade	Number of Students
A	8
B	15
C	20
D	5
F	2

a. Make a bar graph that shows the frequency of each letter grade.

b. Compute the *relative frequency* of each letter grade.

c. Make a bar graph that shows the relative frequencies.

d. Compare the two bar graphs. What do you notice about the shapes of the two distributions?

e. The teacher wants to predict about how many students might earn a letter grade of C in another math class. Should the teacher use frequency or relative frequency to help her make a prediction? Explain.

In this Investigation, you developed strategies to compare two or more distributions with equal or unequal amounts of data. The following questions will help you summarize what you have learned.

Think about these questions. Discuss your ideas with other students and your teacher. Then write a summary of your findings in your notebook.

1. **a.** A new term is used in this Investigation: *sample*. **What** do you think *sample* means?

    b. Suppose you have data from a 7th-grade class. The data are answers to the questions:

    • What is your favorite movie?

    • How many movies do you watch per week?

      i. Which statistics can you use to summarize the results of the data?

      ii. How could you use the data to predict the number of students in the entire 7th grade who would say they watch two movies per week?

2. **a. How** do graphs of distributions help you compare data sets?

    b. How do measures of center help you compare data sets?

    c. How do measures of spread help you compare data sets?

3. **When** does it make sense to compare groups using counts, or frequencies? When does it make sense to compare groups using percents, or relative frequencies? Explain.

Common Core Mathematical Practices

As you worked on the Problems in this Investigation, you used prior knowledge to make sense of them. You also applied Mathematical Practices to solve the Problems. Think back over your work, the ways you thought about the Problems, and how you used Mathematical Practices.

Sophie described her thoughts in the following way:

Sometimes, knowing the mean is not enough when you want to compare data sets. You have to get MAD!

The MAD (mean absolute deviation) is how much, on average, data values in a data set differ from the mean. When there are only a few data values, you can do the work by hand.

In Problem 1.2, the mean amount collected by Team 1 was $35. We found the difference between each member's amount and the mean. We added the differences $(10 + 6 + 2 + 0 + 8 + 10 = 36)$. Then we divided the sum by the total number of team members $(36 \div 6 = 6)$. The MAD for Team 1 was $6. So, on average, the data values were $6 less than or greater than the mean of $35.

For larger data sets, you can use special calculators. We noticed that more consistent data sets had smaller MADs.

....

Common Core Standards for Mathematical Practice
MP6 Attend to precision.

- What other Mathematical Practices can you identify in Sophie's reasoning?

- Describe a Mathematical Practice that you and your classmates used to solve a different Problem in this Investigation.

Choosing a Sample From a Population

Collecting information about the students in your math class, such as their favorite foods or activities, would be fairly easy. On the other hand, collecting information about all the middle-school students in your state would be very difficult.

To make collecting information on a large group, or *population*, easier, you can collect data from a small part, or **sample**, of that population. Depending on how the sample is selected, it may be possible to use the data to make predictions or draw conclusions about an entire population. The challenge is to choose a sample that accurately represents the population as a whole.

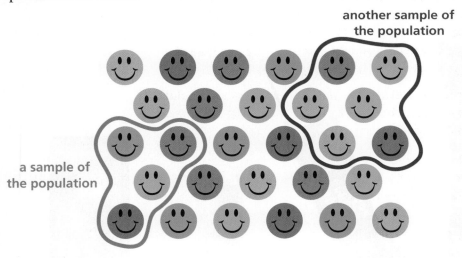

another sample of the population

a sample of the population

Common Core State Standards

7.SP.A.1 Understand that statistics can be used to gain information about a population by examining a sample of the population; generalizations about a population from a sample are valid only if the sample is representative of that population. Understand that random sampling tends to produce representative samples and support valid inferences.

7.SP.A.2 Use data from a random sample to draw inferences about a population with an unknown characteristic of interest. Generate multiple samples (or simulated samples) of the same size to gauge the variation in estimates or predictions.

Also 7.RP.A.3, 7.SP.C.7, 7.SP.C.7a

Consider this information:

> In the United States, over 75% of teens have cell phones. Almost half of the teens who own cell phones own smartphones. So, more than 35% of all teens own smartphones, compared to 23% in 2011.
>
> From 2009 to 2011, the median number of daily texts teens sent rose from 50 to 60. Texting among older teens, ages 14–17, increased from 60 texts to 100 texts per day during that two-year span.

- How could the groups reporting this information know about the activities of all the teenagers in the United States?

- Do you think these facts were gathered from every teenager in the population? Why or why not?

Did You Know?

Thirty years ago, the first "mobile" phones were car phones that weighed over 20 pounds. Early cell phones weighed just under two pounds and cost almost $4,000 (that's roughly $9,200 in today's dollars). Today, smartphones generally weigh about 4 ounces and cost less than $1,000.

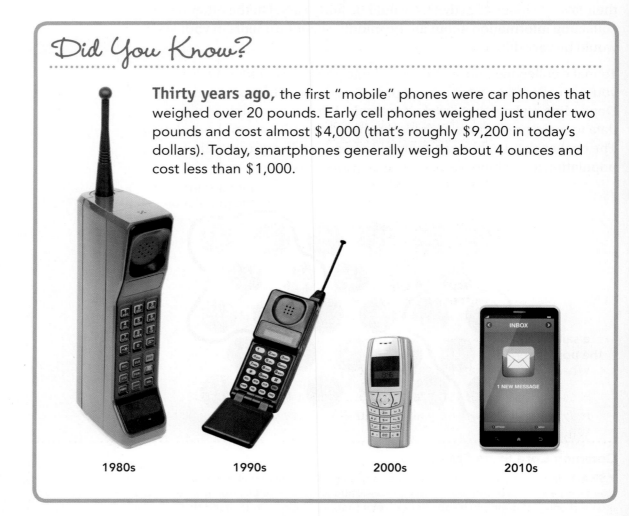

| 1980s | 1990s | 2000s | 2010s |

Samples and Populations

2.1 Asking About Honesty
Using a Sample to Draw Conclusions

Suppose a national magazine asks its readers to respond to the questions below about honesty. Readers take the survey on the magazine's Web site.

HONESTY SURVEY

If This Happened to You

1. What would you do if you found someone's wallet on the street?
a. Try to return it to the owner
b. Return it, but keep the money
c. Keep the wallet and the money

2. What would you do if a cashier mistakenly gave you $10 extra in change?
a. Tell the cashier about the error
b. Say nothing and keep the cash

3. Would you cheat on an exam if you were sure you wouldn't get caught?
a. Yes   b. No

4. Would you download music from the Internet illegally instead of buying the music?
a. Yes   b. No

5. Do you feel that you are an honest person in most situations?
a. Yes   b. No

- What is the population for the Honesty Survey?

- Is asking readers to volunteer their answers a good way for the magazine to draw conclusions about the honesty of the population? Why or why not?

Problem 2.1

A A **sampling plan** is a strategy for choosing a sample from a population. What is the population for the Honesty Survey? What is the sample? How was the sample chosen from the population?

B Suppose 5,280 people completed the survey.

1. For the first question: 3,960 people said they would try to return the wallet to the owner; 792 said they would return the wallet but keep the money; and 528 said they would keep the wallet and the money. What is the relative frequency of each response?

2. For the second question: 4,752 said they would tell the cashier about the error. What is the relative frequency of respondents who said they would tell the cashier about the error?

3. For the third question: 4,224 people answered "No." What is the relative frequency of respondents said they would *not* cheat on an exam?

4. For the fourth question: 1,584 people answered "Yes." What is the relative frequency of respondents who said they would *not* download music illegally from the Internet?

C 1. Make a table or graph that shows the relative frequencies of "honest" and "dishonest" answers for each of the first four questions of the Honesty Survey.

2. Use your table or graph to analyze the responses to the four survey questions. What conclusions can you draw about people's behavior? Explain.

D Use the survey results in Question B and your answers to Question C. Suppose the United States population is about 314 million.

1. Estimate how many people in the United States would say that they would not cheat on an exam.

2. Estimate how many people in the United States would say that they would not download music illegally from the Internet.

Problem **2.1** *continued*

E 1. Do you think this sample of 5,280 people accurately represents the population of the United States? Why or why not?

2. Suppose you were asked to revise the sampling plan for this survey. How could you make sure that the sample more accurately represents the U.S. population?

A C E Homework starts on page 45.

2.2 Selecting a Sample
Different Kinds of Samples

Drawing accurate conclusions about a population based on a sample can be complicated. When you choose a sample, it should be *representative* of the population. This means the sample must have characteristics similar to those of the population. Not all samples are **representative samples.**

Suppose you are doing research on students at your school. You plan to ask these questions:

> • How many hours of sleep do you get each school night?
> • How many movies do you watch each week?

If your school has many students, it might be difficult to gather and analyze data from every student.

• Are these questions clear enough to allow you to collect good data? Why or why not?

• How might you select a sample of your school population to survey?

Problem 2.2

Ms. Ruiz's class is conducting a survey about the number of hours students spend sleeping and the number of hours they spend watching movies. The class divides into four groups. Each group devises a plan for sampling the school population.

I'm surveying the students on my bus.

Group 1

I am surveying every fourth person in the lunch line.

Group 2

We need student volunteers for our survey.

Group 3

By rolling numbered solids, we'll generate student ID numbers for the survey.

Group 4

Problem **2.2** *continued*

A What are the advantages and disadvantages of each sampling plan?

B Which plan do you think will collect the most accurate data to represent students in the whole school? Explain.

C The four sampling plans are examples of common sampling methods.

  1. Group 1's plan is an example of **convenience sampling**. What do you think convenience sampling is? Describe another sampling plan using convenience sampling.

  2. Group 2's plan is an example of **systematic sampling**. What do you think systematic sampling is? Describe another sampling plan using systematic sampling.

  3. Group 3's plan is an example of **voluntary-response sampling**. What do you think voluntary-response sampling is? Describe another sampling plan using voluntary-response sampling.

  4. Group 4's plan is an example of **random sampling**. What do you think random sampling is? Describe another sampling plan using random sampling.

D **1.** Jahmal thinks that Group 1, Group 2, and Group 3 devised sampling plans that might not give representative samples. Do you agree or disagree? Explain.

  2. Jahmal comes up with a new plan. He thinks each teacher should select one boy and one girl and ask them the survey questions. There are four teachers for each grade (Grades 6–8), so they would end up with a sample of 24 students.

   i. What type of sampling plan is this?

   ii. Will it give a representative sample?

   iii. Do you like Jahmal's plan? Explain. If you do not like Jahmal's plan, how would you change it?

 Homework starts on page 45.

2.3 Choosing Random Samples
Comparing Samples Using Center and Spread

In most cases, a good sampling plan is one that gives each member of the population the same chance of being selected. To do this, you may use concepts from probability, such as *equally likely* outcomes.

A random sampling plan gives each member of a population an equally likely chance of being included in the sample. The resulting sample is called a random sample.

To select a random sample from a population of 100 students, you can use spinners to generate pairs of random digits.

- How does using the two spinners help you select a random sample from a population of 100 students?

- What two-digit numbers can you generate with the spinners?

- How can you make sure Student 100 has an equally likely chance of being included in your sample?

- What ideas from probability are you using?

There are many other ways to select a random sample of students. For example, you could roll two 10-sided numbered solids or generate random numbers with your calculator.

- What other strategies could you use?

The table on the next page shows data collected from a 7th-grade class. The data include the number of hours of sleep each student got the previous night and the number of movies each student watched the previous week.

- How can you use statistics from a random sample to draw conclusions about the entire population of 7th-grade students in the school?

Responses to Grade 7 Movie and Sleep Survey

Student	Sleep Last Night (h)	Movies Last Week (no. of)	Student	Sleep Last Night (h)	Movies Last Week (no. of)	Student	Sleep Last Night (h)	Movies Last Week (no. of)
01	11.5	14	35	6.5	5	68	5.5	0
02	2.0	8	36	9.3	1	69	10.5	7
03	7.7	3	37	8.2	3	70	7.5	1
04	9.3	1	38	7.3	3	71	7.8	0
05	7.1	16	39	7.4	6	72	7.3	1
06	7.5	1	40	8.5	7	73	9.3	2
07	8.0	4	41	5.5	17	74	9.0	1
08	7.8	1	42	6.5	3	75	8.7	1
09	8.0	13	43	7.0	5	76	8.5	3
10	8.0	15	44	8.5	2	77	9.0	1
11	9.0	1	45	9.3	4	78	8.0	1
12	9.2	10	46	8.0	15	79	8.0	4
13	8.5	5	47	8.5	10	80	6.5	0
14	6.0	15	48	6.2	11	81	8.0	0
15	6.5	10	49	11.8	10	82	9.0	8
16	8.3	2	50	9.0	4	83	8.0	0
17	7.4	2	51	5.0	4	84	7.0	0
18	11.2	3	52	6.5	5	85	9.0	6
19	7.3	1	53	8.5	2	86	7.3	0
20	8.0	0	54	9.1	15	87	9.0	3
21	7.8	1	55	7.5	2	88	7.5	5
22	7.8	1	56	8.5	1	89	8.0	0
23	9.2	2	57	8.0	2	90	7.5	6
24	7.5	0	58	7.0	7	91	8.0	4
25	8.8	1	59	8.4	10	92	9.0	4
26	8.5	0	60	9.5	1	93	7.0	0
27	9.0	0	61	7.3	5	94	8.0	3
28	8.5	0	62	7.3	4	95	8.3	3
29	8.2	2	63	8.5	3	96	8.3	14
30	7.8	2	64	9.0	3	97	7.8	5
31	8.0	2	65	9.0	4	98	8.5	1
32	7.3	8	66	7.3	5	99	8.3	3
33	6.0	5	67	5.7	0	100	7.5	2
34	7.5	5						

Problem 2.3

In this Problem, you will choose a sample and then represent the data with a line plot and with a box plot. You will compare your sample's distribution with your classmates' distributions. Your class should decide on a scale for the line plot and box plot before starting.

(A) **1.** Select a random sample of 30 students from the table on the previous page. Your sample should include 30 different students. If you select a student who is already in your sample, select another.

2. For each student in your sample, record the number of hours slept and the number of movies watched.

(B) **1.** Make a line plot showing the number of movies watched by your sample.

2. **a.** Locate the mean.

　　b. Describe the shape of the distribution.

3. Find the range and MAD. Describe the variability of the number of movies watched by students in your sample.

4. Compare your sample distribution with those of your classmates. Describe any similarities or differences.

5. What can you conclude about the number of movies the population of 7th-grade students watched last week based on all the samples selected by your class? Explain.

(C) **1.** Find the *five-number summary* of the number of hours slept for your sample. Make a box-and-whisker plot of the data in your sample.

2. Describe the shape of the distribution.

3. Find the range and IQR. Describe the variability of the number of hours slept for the students in your sample.

4. Compare your sample distribution with those of your classmates. Describe any similarities or differences.

5. What can you conclude about the number of hours the population of 7th-grade students slept last night based on all the samples selected by your class? Explain.

 Homework starts on page 45.

2.4 Growing Samples
What Size Sample to Use?

In Problem 2.3, you used statistics from random samples to estimate the number of hours slept and the number of movies watched by 100 students.

- Are you able to make good estimates with less work by selecting smaller samples?
- How does sample size relate to the accuracy of statistical estimates?

Problem 2.4

A Use the population of 100 students from Problem 2.3. Select a random sample of 5 students and a random sample of 10 students. Record the number of hours slept and the number of movies watched for each student. **Note:** You should select a new set of students for each sample, but one or more students may happen to appear in both samples.

B Use all three samples (the 5-student sample and the 10-student sample from Question A, and the 30-student sample from Problem 2.3) to answer the questions below.

1. For each sample size (5, 10, and 30), find the mean and median number of hours slept. Find the mean and median number of movies watched. Find the IQR and the MAD of each data set.

2. Record the means, the medians, the IQRs, and the MADs in a class chart. Record the summary statistics of your classmates' samples as well.

continued on the next page >

Problem 2.4 *continued*

C 1. Use the class data about the mean number of movies watched. For each sample size (5, 10, and 30 students), make a line plot displaying the *means* of the samples. You will have three line plots, each showing how the means vary across the samples. These are called **sampling distributions**. Compare the three sampling distributions by describing the variability in each distribution.

2. The mean number of movies watched for the population of 100 students is 4.22 movies. Write a paragraph describing how close the means of samples of different sizes are to the mean of the population.

D 1. Use the class data about the median number of movies watched. For each sample size, make a line plot displaying the *medians* of the samples. You will have three line plots, each showing how the medians vary across the samples. Compare the three sampling distributions by describing the variability in each distribution.

2. The median number of movies watched for the population of 100 students is 3 movies. Write a paragraph describing how close the medians of samples of different sizes are to the median of the population.

E For the population of 100 students, the mean number of hours slept is 7.96 hours, and the median is 8 hours.

Follow the steps you used in Questions C and D to analyze the distribution of means and medians of samples of different sizes. Discuss how close the means and medians of samples of different sizes are to the mean and median of the whole population for the number of hours slept.

F Suppose each student in your class chose a sample of 50 students and found the means and medians of the data for the number of hours slept and the number of movies watched. What would you expect the line plots of these means and medians to look like? Explain.

G Use the class chart of summary statistics. What patterns do you see in the measures of spread for the three different sample sizes? Explain why these patterns make sense.

A C E Homework starts on page 45.

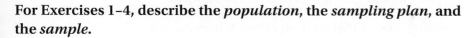

Applications

For Exercises 1–4, describe the *population*, the *sampling plan*, and the *sample*.

1. A magazine for teenagers asks its readers to write in with information about how they solve personal problems.

2. An 8th-grade class wants to find out how much time middle-school students spend on the telephone each day. Students in the class keep a record of the amount of time they spend on the phone each day for a week.

3. Ms. Darnell's class wants to estimate the number of soft drinks middle-school students drink each day. They obtain a list of students in the school and write each name on a card. They put the cards in a box and select the names of 40 students to survey.

4. The newspaper below gives information about how adults feel about global warming. The editors of the school paper want to find out how students feel about this issue. They select 26 students for their survey—one whose name begins with A, one whose name begins with B, one whose name begins with C, and so on.

A middle school has 350 students. One math class decides to investigate how many hours a typical student in the school spent doing homework last week. Several students suggest sampling plans. For Exercises 5–8, name the type of sampling plan. Then tell whether you think the sampling plan would give a representative sample.

5. Zak suggests surveying every third student on each homeroom class list.

6. Kwang-Hee suggests putting 320 white beans and 30 red beans in a bag. Each student would draw a bean as he or she enters the auditorium for an assembly. The 30 students who draw red beans will be surveyed.

7. Ushio suggests that each student in the class survey everyone in his or her English class.

8. Kirby suggests putting surveys on a table at lunch and asking students to return completed questionnaires at the end of the day.

9. A radio host asked her listeners to call in to express their opinions about a local election. What kind of sampling plan is she using? Do you think the results of this survey could be used to describe the opinions of all the show's listeners? Explain.

Manufacturers often conduct quality-control tests on samples of their products. For Exercises 10–13, describe a random sampling plan you would recommend to the company. Justify your recommendation.

10. A toy company produces 5,000 video-game systems each day.

11. A music company manufactures a total of 200,000 compact discs for about 100 recording artists each day.

12. A fireworks company produces over 1,500 rockets each day.

13. A bottling company produces 25,000 bottles of spring water each day.

14. Use the table from Problem 2.3.

    a. Suppose you select the first 30 students for a sample. A second student selects the next 30 students for a different sample, and so on. Will these samples be representative? Explain.

    b. You select students 1, 5, 9, 13, 17, 21, 25, . . . for your sample. A second student chooses students 2, 6, 10, 14, 18, 22, 26, . . . for his sample. A third student chooses students 3, 7, 11, 15, 19, 23, 27, . . . for her sample, and so on. Will this result in representative samples? Explain.

15. **a.** The homecoming committee wants to estimate how many students will attend the homecoming dance. It does not, however, want to ask every student in the school. Describe a method the committee could use to select a sample of students to survey.

    b. Describe how the committee could use the results of its survey to predict the number of students who will attend the dance.

16. Use the graph below. About how many more hours per day does a typical newborn sleep than a typical 10- to 13-year-old?

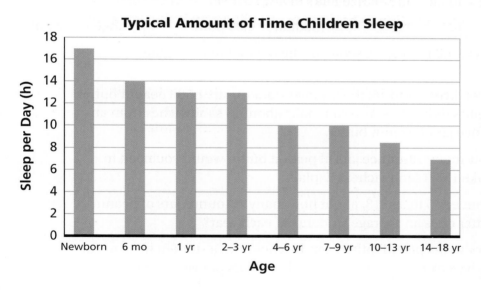

Typical Amount of Time Children Sleep

17. Suppose you want to survey students in your school to find out how many hours they sleep each night. Which would be the best sample size: 5 students, 10 students, or 30 students? Explain.

Connections

18. The scoreboard below displays Ella's diving scores from a recent competition. One score cannot be read.

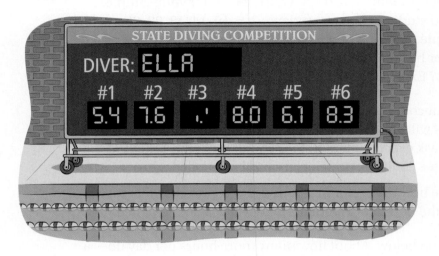

These statistics summarize Ella's diving scores:

mean = 6.75 points   median = 6.85 points   range = 3.2 points

What was Ella's missing score for the competition? Explain.

19. Between ages 5 and 18, the average student eats 1,500 peanut butter and jelly sandwiches. You can make about 15 sandwiches from an 18-ounce jar of peanut butter.

   a. How many 18-ounce jars of peanut butter would you need to make 1,500 sandwiches? Explain.

   b. From age 5 to age 18, about how many 18-ounce jars of peanut butter does an average student eat each year?

   c. How many peanut butter sandwiches does a student need to eat each week to consume the number of jars per year from part (b)?

For Exercises 20–22, use the two dot plots below. The dot plots show the number of hours students spent doing homework on Monday.

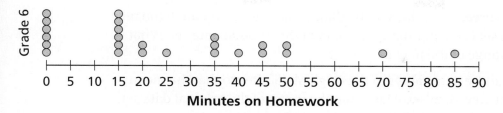

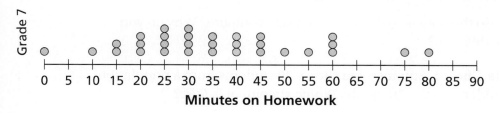

20. Find the median homework times. Copy and complete the table below.

Time Spent on Homework (minutes)

Grade	Mean	Median	MAD
6	25.8	▪	18.56
7	36.13	▪	14.53

21. **a.** For each grade, describe the variability in the distribution of homework times. Use what you know about the distribution's shape and the MAD.

   b. Use statistics to compare the times 6th graders spent doing homework to the times 7th graders spent doing homework.

22. Could these data be used to describe the time spent on homework on a typical school night by a typical student in each grade? Explain.

23. Consider the following data set: 20, 22, 23, 23, 24, 24, and 25.

    a. Find the mean and the range of the values.

    b. Add three data values to the data set so that the mean of the new data set is greater than the mean of the original data set. What is the range of the new data set?

    c. Add three data values to the original data set so that the mean of the new data set is less than the mean of the original data set. What is the range of the new data set?

    d. How do the ranges of the three data sets compare? Why do you think this is so?

24. **Multiple Choice** Suppose you survey 30 students from a population of 150 students in the 7th grade. Which statement is *false*?

    A. The ratio of those sampled to those not sampled is 30 to 120.

    B. One out of every five people in the population was sampled.

    C. Twenty-five percent of the students in the population were sampled.

    D. One-fifth of the students in the population were sampled.

25. There are 350 students in a school. Ms. Cabral's class surveys two random samples of students to find out how many went to camp last summer. The results are below.

    Sample 1: 8 of 25 attended camp.

    Sample 2: 7 of 28 attended camp.

    a. Use the results from Sample 1. What fraction of the students in the school do you think attended camp? How many students attended camp?

    b. Use the results from Sample 2. What fraction of the students in the school do you think attended camp? How many students attended camp?

    c. Which sample concludes that the greater fraction of students attended camp?

    d. One of Ms. Cabral's students says, "We were careful to choose our samples at random. Why did the two samples give us different conclusions?" How would you answer the student's question?

Use the following information for Exercises 26–31.

Annie's teacher starts each class with the names of all the students in a container. There are 12 girls and 6 boys in the class.

The teacher pulls out names at random to choose students to present answers. After choosing a name, the teacher sets the name aside. At the end of class, the teacher replaces all the names in the container. So, each student's name has a chance of being chosen the next day.

26. What is the probability Annie will be the first student chosen on Monday?

27. What is the probability Annie will be the first student chosen on Tuesday?

28. What is the probability Annie will be the first student chosen on both Monday and Tuesday?

29. What is the probability the first student chosen on a given day will be a girl?

30. Suppose Annie is chosen first. What is the probability that the next student selected will be another girl?

31. Suppose the teacher plans to choose six students during one class. Would you be surprised if only two girls were chosen? Explain.

Use the following information for Exercises 32 and 33. Alyssa wants to know what students think about replacing the candy in two vending machines in the cafeteria with more healthful snacks. Alyssa obtains a list of student names, grouped by grade, with the girls listed first in each grade.

There are 300 6th graders, 300 7th graders, and 200 8th graders. Half of the students in each grade are girls.

32. Alyssa chooses 3 different students at random from the list of 800 students.

   a. What is the probability that the first choice is a girl? The second choice is a girl? The third choice is a girl?

   b. What is the probability that Alyssa chooses three girls?

33. Alyssa decides to choose one person *from each grade* at random.

   a. What is the probability that the 6th-grade choice is a girl?

   b. What is the probability that she chooses three girls?

For Exercises 34–38, use the table below. Alyssa chooses one girl and one boy from each grade. She asks each, "Which would you prefer, a machine with healthful snacks or a machine with candy?"

Vending Machine Preferences

	Grade 6	Grade 7	Grade 8
Girl	healthful snack	healthful snack	healthful snack
Boy	candy	candy	healthful snack

34. How many 6th-grade students do you think prefer a machine with healthful snacks?

35. How many students in the whole school do you think prefer a machine with healthful snacks?

36. What is the probability that a student chosen at random from the whole school is an 8th grader who prefers a machine with healthful snacks?

37. What advice would you give Alyssa's principal about Alyssa's data and the two vending machines? Explain.

38. Alyssa's principal polls all 800 students and finds that 600 prefer a machine with healthful snacks.

   a. What is the probability that a student selected at random prefers a machine with healthful snacks?

   b. What is the probability that a student selected at random is a girl who prefers a machine with healthful snacks?

   c. What is the probability that a student selected at random is a boy who prefers a machine with healthful snacks?

   d. What advice would you give the principal about the data collected and the vending machines?

Extensions

39. Television stations, radio stations, and newspapers often use polls to predict the winners of elections long before the votes are cast. What factors might cause a pre-election poll to be inaccurate?

40. Political parties often write and then conduct their own pre-election polls to find out what voters think about their campaign and their candidates. How might such a poll be biased?

41. **a.** Polls conducted prior to presidential elections commonly use samples of about 1,000 eligible voters. Suppose there are 207 million eligible voters in the United States. About what percent of eligible voters are in a sample of 1,000?

   b. How do you think this small sample is chosen so that the results will predict the winner with reasonable accuracy? Consider which groups within the total population need to be represented, such as adults 65 years or older.

Did You Know?

How do pollsters decide whom to contact? When pollsters take phone polls, they use random sampling techniques to choose voters from the total voting population. Internet polls, in most cases, exclude households without Internet access. Most online polls are also completed by people who choose to participate.

In this Investigation, you learned about sampling techniques. You also drew conclusions about a population by examining data from random samples. The following questions will help you summarize what you have learned.

Think about these questions. Discuss your ideas with other students and your teacher. Then, write a summary of your findings in your notebook.

1. **Why** are data often collected from a sample rather than from an entire population?

2. **Describe** four plans for selecting a sample from a population. Discuss the advantages and disadvantages of each plan.

3. a. **How** are random samples different from convenience, voluntary-response, and systematic samples?

    b. **Why** is random sampling preferable to the other sampling plans?

    c. **Describe** three plans for selecting a random sample from a given population. **What** are the advantages and disadvantages of each plan?

4. Suppose you select several random samples of size 30 from the same population.

    a. When you compare the samples to each other, **what** similarities and differences would you expect to find among the measures of center and spread?

    b. When you compare the samples to the larger population, **what** similarities and differences would you expect to find among the measures of center and spread?

5. **How** has your idea of the term *sample* changed from what you wrote in Mathematical Reflections, Investigation 1?

Common Core Mathematical Practices

As you worked on the Problems in this Investigation, you used prior knowledge to make sense of them. You also applied Mathematical Practices to solve the Problems. Think back over your work, the ways you thought about the Problems, and how you used Mathematical Practices.

Nick described his thoughts in the following way:

In Problem 2.4, I was able to use data from all of the samples that my classmates had gathered. Instead of collecting multiple samples myself, we compiled all of our class data in one big chart.

I could use the information from all of the samples to draw conclusions about the means and medians of the larger population's data. The more data I could use, the more confident I was that my conclusions about the whole population were accurate.

Common Core Standards for Mathematical Practice

MP7 Look for and make use of structure.

- What other Mathematical Practices can you identify in Nick's reasoning?

- Describe a Mathematical Practice that you and your classmates used to solve a different Problem in this Investigation.

3

Using Samples to Draw Conclusions

There are many different possible samples in any population. You can use a random sampling plan to help you choose your sample fairly. In general, large random samples are more representative than small random samples or samples chosen with other sampling methods.

3.1 Solving an Archeological Mystery
Comparing Samples Using Box Plots

Archeologists study past civilizations by excavating ancient settlements. They examine the artifacts of the people who lived there.

Common Core State Standards

7.SP.A.1 Understand that statistics can be used to gain information about a population by examining a sample of the population; generalizations about a population from a sample are valid only if the sample is representative of that population. Understand that random sampling tends to produce representative samples and support valid inferences.

7.SP.B.3 Informally assess the degree of visual overlap of two numerical data distributions with similar variabilities, measuring the difference between the centers by expressing it as a multiple of a measure of variability.

Also 7.RP.A.2, 7.NS.A.1, 7.NS.A.1b, 7.SP.A.2, 7.SP.B.4, 7.SP.C.5, and 7.SP.C.7b

On digs in southeastern Montana and north-central Wyoming, archeologists discovered the remains of two Native American settlements. They found a number of arrowheads at each site. The archeologists hoped to use the arrowheads to estimate the time period in which each site was inhabited.

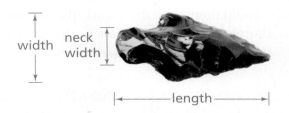

The tables below give the lengths, widths, and neck widths of the arrowheads the archeologists found. The sets of data are samples from different populations of arrowheads from two different time periods.

Site I: 15 Arrowheads

Length (mm)	Width (mm)	Neck Width (mm)
24	19	8
27	19	10
29	19	11
29	22	12
31	16	12
31	32	16
37	23	11
38	22	12
38	26	14
40	25	16
45	22	11
45	28	15
55	22	13
62	26	14
63	29	18

SOURCE: *Plains Anthropologist*

Site II: 37 Arrowheads

Length (mm)	Width (mm)	Neck Width (mm)	Length (mm)	Width (mm)	Neck Width (mm)
13	10	6	24	13	8
15	11	7	24	13	8
16	12	8	24	14	10
16	13	7	24	15	9
17	15	9	24	15	8
18	12	10	25	13	7
19	12	8	25	13	7
19	13	9	25	15	10
20	12	7	25	24	7
20	12	9	26	14	10
21	11	7	26	14	11
22	13	9	26	15	11
22	13	9	27	14	8
22	13	8	28	11	6
22	14	10	28	13	9
23	14	9	32	12	8
23	15	9	42	16	11
24	11	8	43	14	9
24	12	7			

To help them with their work, the archeologists also used samples of arrowhead data from four other settlement sites. The data from those sites are on this page and on the next page.

The archeologists knew that the Big Goose Creek and Wortham Shelter sites were settled between A.D. 500 and A.D. 1600.

Big Goose Creek: 52 Arrowheads

Length (mm)	Width (mm)	Neck Width (mm)	Length (mm)	Width (mm)	Neck Width (mm)
16	13	9	26	12	12
16	14	10	26	14	9
17	13	8	26	16	10
17	13	10	27	13	9
18	12	7	27	13	9
18	12	8	27	14	9
18	13	7	27	14	9
18	15	11	27	17	13
19	11	8	28	10	5
20	11	6	28	13	7
20	12	8	28	13	8
21	11	7	28	15	9
21	12	7	29	15	8
21	12	9	30	11	7
22	12	9	30	13	8
22	13	8	30	14	8
22	13	10	30	14	8
23	13	8	30	14	9
23	13	9	30	15	11
23	14	9	31	12	8
24	14	9	33	13	7
24	14	11	33	15	9
25	13	7	34	15	9
25	13	8	35	14	10
25	14	8	39	18	12
26	11	8	40	14	8

SOURCE: *Plains Anthropologist*

Wortham Shelter: 45 Arrowheads

Length (mm)	Width (mm)	Neck Width (mm)
18	11	8
19	12	9
19	14	10
19	14	10
19	16	14
20	13	8
20	14	10
20	15	11
22	12	9
22	14	8
23	13	11
23	14	11
23	15	11
24	12	9
24	13	10
25	14	8
25	14	10
25	15	10
25	15	10
25	15	12
26	13	9
26	13	10
26	15	12
27	14	8
27	14	10
27	15	11
28	13	11
28	14	10
28	16	12
29	13	10
29	14	9
29	14	9
29	17	12
30	14	11
30	16	9
30	17	11
31	13	10
31	14	10
31	14	11
31	16	12
31	17	12
32	14	7
32	15	10
35	18	14
42	18	7

The archeologists knew that the Laddie Creek/Dead Indian Creek and Kobold/Buffalo Creek sites were settled between 4000 B.C. and A.D. 500.

- How could you use the data to estimate the length and width of a typical arrowhead from each time period?

- How could you use the data to determine the settlement periods for the unknown sites?

Laddie Creek/ Dead Indian Creek: 18 Arrowheads

Length (mm)	Width (mm)	Neck Width (mm)
25	18	13
27	20	13
27	20	14
29	14	11
29	20	13
30	23	13
31	18	11
32	16	10
32	19	10
35	20	15
37	17	13
38	17	14
39	18	15
40	18	11
41	15	11
42	22	12
44	18	13
52	21	16

Kobold/Buffalo Creek: 52 Arrowheads

Length (mm)	Width (mm)	Neck Width (mm)	Length (mm)	Width (mm)	Neck Width (mm)
25	18	15	45	22	13
30	17	12	46	17	13
30	19	15	46	20	14
31	16	13	46	23	14
31	17	12	47	19	13
32	20	13	47	20	12
32	22	17	47	22	13
32	23	18	49	20	14
35	19	11	50	21	13
35	22	14	50	23	15
37	18	12	50	23	16
37	21	11	51	18	10
38	18	9	52	17	12
38	24	15	52	22	15
39	21	14	52	24	16
40	19	15	54	24	13
40	20	12	56	19	12
40	20	13	56	21	15
40	21	12	56	25	13
41	21	13	57	21	15
42	22	14	61	19	12
42	22	15	64	21	13
44	20	11	66	20	15
44	20	12	67	21	13
44	25	14	71	24	13
45	20	13	78	26	12

Problem 3.1

The archeologists thought that Native Americans inhabiting the same area of the country during the same time period would have similar tools.

A **1.** For each known site and each unknown site, find the five-number summary of the arrowhead-length data. Then draw a box-and-whisker plot of each distribution.

2. Use your answers to part (1). Compare the lengths of the arrowheads found at the unknown sites with the lengths of the arrowheads found at the known sites.

   a. During which time period (4000 B.C.–A.D. 500 or A.D. 500–A.D. 1600) do you think Site I was settled? Explain how your statistics and box plots support your answers.

   b. During which time period do you think Site II was settled? Explain how your statistics and box plots support your answers.

B **1.** For each known site and each unknown site, find the five-number summary of the arrowhead-width data. Then draw a box plot of each distribution.

2. Do the box plots displaying data about arrowhead widths support your answers to Question A, part (2)? Explain.

C Suppose the archeologists had collected only a few arrowheads from each unknown site. Might they have reached a different conclusion? Explain.

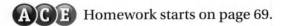 Homework starts on page 69.

3.2 Comparing Heights of Basketball Players
Using Means and MADs

Variability occurs naturally in all samples of a population. Distributions of two different samples will not be identical. When you compare two samples, you need to decide whether the samples differ more than what you would expect from natural variability.

The dot plots below show the heights of a random sample of 32 male professional basketball players and the heights of a random sample of 32 female professional basketball players.

Heights of Male Professional Basketball Players

Mean: 199.9063
MAD: 8.7871

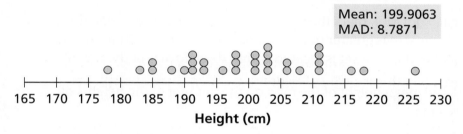

Heights of Female Professional Basketball Players

Mean: 183.8125
MAD: 7.0625

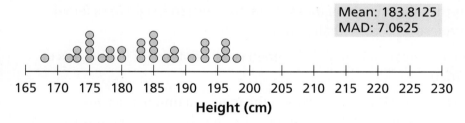

- Do these samples give enough evidence to conclude that the population of male professional basketball players is taller than the population of female professional basketball players? Or is the difference you see in these samples just due to natural variation?

In Investigation 1, you looked at how the mean and MAD are related. You found that, in many distributions, most of the data are located within two MADs of the mean.

Problem 3.2

Use the dot plots of professional basketball players' heights on the previous page.

(A) Compare the means of the two sets of data. Compare the variabilities of the two sets of data.

(B) **1.** On a copy of each dot plot, mark the locations of two MADs less than the mean and two MADs greater than the mean.

 2. For each distribution, what percent of the data set is located within two MADs of the mean?

 3. For each dot plot, mark the locations of three MADs less than the mean and three MADs greater than the mean. For each distribution, what percent of the data set is located within three MADs of the mean?

(C) **1.** Mark the mean height of the men on the dot plot of the heights of the women.

 a. Use the MAD of the heights of the women as a unit of measure. Within how many MADs of the mean height of the women is the mean height of the men?

 b. Is the mean height of the men an unexpected height for a female professional basketball player? Explain.

 2. Mark the mean height of the women on the dot plot of the heights of the men.

 a. Use the MAD of the heights of the men as a unit of measure. Within how many MADs of the mean height of the men is the mean height of the women?

 b. Is the mean height of the women an unexpected height for a male professional basketball player? Explain your reasoning.

 3. Do these sample distributions provide enough evidence to draw conclusions about the heights of the populations from which the samples were drawn? Explain.

Problem 3.2 *continued*

D The dot plot below shows a distribution of heights for a sample of professional basketball players. Do you think this distribution shows a random sample of men or a random sample of women? Explain.

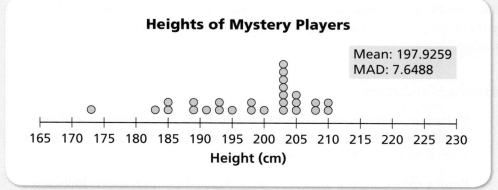

Heights of Mystery Players

Mean: 197.9259
MAD: 7.6488

Height (cm)

A C E Homework starts on page 69.

3.3 Five Chocolate Chips in Every Cookie
Using Sampling in a Simulation

Jeff and Hadiya work at the Custom Cookie Counter. Their advertising slogan is "Five giant chips in every cookie!"

One day, a customer complains that her cookie only has three chocolate chips. Jeff thinks she must have miscounted because he mixes 60 chips into the dough of each batch of a dozen cookies. Jeff and Hadiya examine a batch of cookies fresh from the oven. The picture at the right shows what they see.

• How might you correct Jeff's reasoning about how many chocolate chips to add to each batch of cookie dough?

• What advice would you give to Jeff and Hadiya to help them solve this quality-control problem?

Hadiya wants to figure out how many chocolate chips they should add to each batch of dough. She wants to be fairly confident that each cookie will have five chips. She simulates the situation by using random sampling. When Hadiya **simulates** the quality-control problem, she runs an experiment that models the relevant characteristics of the cookie-dough problem.

Hadiya says, "Think of a batch of dough as 12 cookies packed in a bowl. Each chip that we add to the dough lands in one cookie. There is an equally likely chance that a chip will land in any one of the 12 cookies. We can simulate the situation."

Hadiya's Simulation

- Select integers from 1 to 12 at random to assign chocolate chips to cookies. A "1" means a chip is included in Cookie 1. A "2" means a chip is included in Cookie 2, and so on.

- Keep a tally of where the chips land. Stop when each cookie includes at least five chips.

- The total number of tallied chips will be an estimate of the number of chips needed for each batch.

Jeff extends Hadiya's idea. He says, "Each time we simulate the situation, we might get a different number of chips. For some simulations, some cookies might be loaded with chips before each cookie gets five chips. We need to repeat the experiment enough times to find a typical result."

- What is the typical number of chips needed to have at least five chips in each cookie?

Problem 3.3

A **1.** For each cookie, 1 to 12, what is the theoretical probability of a chip being assigned to that cookie?

2. Describe a method that you can use to give each chip a cookie number. Explain why your method makes it equally likely for each cookie to be assigned a chip.

3. Conduct the simulation Hadiya described. Record your results in a table such as the one below.

Cookie Simulation

Cookie Number	1	2	3	4	5	6	7	8	9	10	11	12
Number of Chips in the Cookie	▪	▪	▪	▪	▪	▪	▪	▪	▪	▪	▪	▪

B Find the total number of chips in your simulated batch of cookie dough.

C Ask each group in your class for the total number of chips in their simulated batches of cookie dough.

1. Make a *histogram* of the class data.

2. Describe your histogram. Explain how you chose the interval size. What does the histogram tell you about the results of the simulations?

3. Make a box-and-whisker plot of the class data.

4. Describe your box plot. What does the box plot tell you about the results of the simulations?

5. Compute the mean and the median of the class data. Compare the mean and the median. What do you notice?

D Jeff and Hadiya want to be sure that most of the cookies they make will have at least five chips. They do not want to waste money, however, by mixing in too many chips. How many chips do you predict they need to use in each batch? Use your answers to Question C to explain your reasoning.

continued on the next page >

Problem **3.3**   *continued*

 1. As a class, discuss your answers to Question D. Choose a number to suggest to Jeff and Hadiya that the whole class agrees on.

2. Use the number of chips your class agreed on.

- As a class, conduct 30 simulations to distribute the recommended number of chips among 12 cookies.

- For each simulation, record whether each of the 12 cookies has at least five chips.

- Organize your information in a table such as the one below.

Trials for Recommended Number of Chips

Simulation Trial Number	Does Each Cookie Have at Least Five Chips?
1	▪
2	▪
3	▪
4	▪
⋮	▪
30	▪

3. What percent of the simulations resulted in at least five chips per cookie?

4. Make a final recommendation. How many chips should Jeff and Hadiya put in each batch? Use your simulation results to justify your choice.

5. Suggest a new advertising slogan for Jeff and Hadiya that might promote their cookies in a more accurate way.

 Homework starts on page 69.

3.4 Estimating a Deer Population
Using Samples to Estimate the Size of a Population

Scientists and environmentalists estimate populations of various animals in particular habitats.

- How can you estimate the deer population of a town, state, or region?

The **capture–tag–recapture method** is one way to estimate a deer population. Biologists capture a sample of deer in a specific area, tag the deer, and then release them. Later, they capture another sample of deer. They count the number of deer with tags and compare that number to the number of deer in the sample. Then, they use their comparison to estimate the number of deer in the area.

You can simulate the capture–tag–recapture method using beans. Think of each bean in a container as a deer. Your job is to estimate the total number of beans without counting them all.

How to Simulate the Capture–Tag–Recapture Method

Capture–Tag

- Remove 100 beans from the container. Mark them with a pen or marker.

- Put the beans back in the container. Gently shake the container to mix the marked and unmarked beans.

Recapture

- Without examining the beans, scoop out a sample from the container. Record the number of marked beans and the number of beans in the sample.

- Return the sample of beans to the container. Mix the beans together again.

- How does the sample of beans you recaptured help you determine how many beans are in the population?

When biologists use the capture–tag–recapture method, they do not collect samples of specific sizes. In this Problem, however, you will collect samples of specific sizes so that you can compare your answers with your classmates' answers.

Problem 3.4

Work with your group to simulate the capture–tag–recapture method.

A **1.** Take a sample of 25 beans. Record the number of marked beans and the number of unmarked beans in a table such as the one below. Use the data to estimate the total number of beans in the container.

Capture–Tag–Recapture Sampling Data

Sample Size	Number of Marked Beans	Number of Unmarked Beans	Estimate of Total Number of Beans
25	■	■	■
50	■	■	■
75	■	■	■
100	■	■	■
125	■	■	■
150	■	■	■

2. Follow the steps you used in part (1) with samples of 50 beans, 75 beans, 100 beans, 125 beans, and 150 beans. Record your data.

3. Describe the strategy you used to estimate the total number of beans in the container.

B Explain why this experiment can be considered a simulation.

C Use the table from Question A. Make a final estimate for the number of total beans in the container. Explain your reasoning.

D Ask each group in your class for their estimates of total number of beans in the container for each sample size.

1. For each sample size, draw a line plot of the data you collected from your class.

2. Explain how the line plots you drew in part (1) might change your final estimate for the total number of beans in the container.

E Use what you have learned from this experiment. How do you think biologists count deer populations?

A C E Homework starts on page 69.

Applications

1. A zookeeper has tracked the weights of many chimpanzees over the years. The box plots below show the weights of two samples of chimpanzees. The top box plot shows a sample of 8-year-old chimpanzees. The bottom box plot shows a sample of 10-year-old chimpanzees.

8-Year-Old Chimpanzees

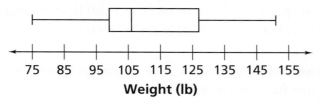

10-Year-Old Chimpanzees

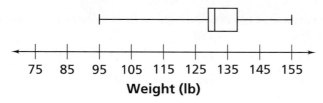

The zoo acquired some chimpanzees from a nearby zoo that was closing. They received a cage of 8-year-old chimpanzees and a cage of 10-year-old chimpanzees. The zoo forgot, however, to keep track of the cages. They weighed the chimpanzees in one cage and graphed the data.

Mystery Chimpanzees

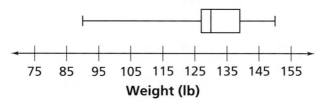

How old are the chimpanzees shown in the distribution above? Explain your reasoning.

2. a. Use the arrowhead tables from Problem 3.1. The tables include the neck widths of the arrowheads from two unknown sites and four known sites. For each of the six sites, calculate the five-number summaries of the neck-width data.

neck width

b. Make a box-and-whisker plot of the neck-width data for each site. You can use the same number line to plot all the box plots.

c. During which time periods do you think Sites I and II were settled? Use your answers to parts (a) and (b) to justify your response.

A sample of students measured their heights, arm spans, and foot lengths. Use the table below for Exercises 3–6.

Student Measurement Data

Gender	Height (cm)	Arm Span (cm)	Foot Length (cm)
F	160	158	25
M	111	113	15
F	160	160	23
F	152	155	23.5
F	146	144	24
F	157	156	24
M	136	135	21
F	143	142	23
M	147	145	20
M	133	133	20
F	153	151	25
M	148	149	23
M	125	123	20
F	150	149	20

3. a. Make a line plot displaying the foot lengths of the female students.

b. What is the mean of the data? The MAD?

c. On your line plot, mark the locations of one MAD and two MADs less than and greater than the mean.

4. a. Make a line plot displaying the foot lengths of the male students.

b. What is the mean of the data? The MAD?

c. On your line plot, mark the locations of one MAD and two MADs less than and greater than the mean.

5. Use your answers to Exercises 3 and 4. Mark the mean male foot length on the line plot of female foot lengths. Is the mean male foot length an unexpected data value for the female line plot? Explain.

6. Use your answers to Exercises 3 and 4. Mark the mean female foot length on the line plot of male foot lengths. Is the mean female foot length an unexpected data value for the male line plot? Explain.

7. The line plots below display the name lengths of a sample of 30 U.S. students and a sample of 30 Chinese students.

Keron and Ethan notice that U.S. names are longer than Chinese names for these samples. Keron thinks this is due to naturally occurring variability. Ethan thinks the differences are too great to be explained only by naturally occurring variability. Do you agree with Keron or with Ethan? Explain.

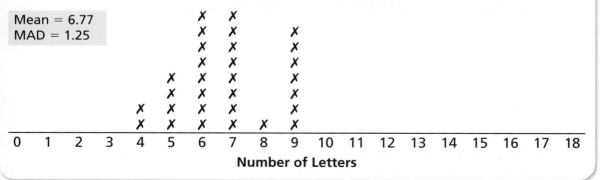

Keisha opens a bag containing 60 chocolate chip cookies. She selects a sample of 20 cookies and counts the chips in each cookie. For Exercises 8 and 9, use Keisha's data below.

Cookie Sample

Cookie Number	Number of Chips	Cookie Number	Number of Chips
1	6	11	8
2	8	12	7
3	8	13	9
4	11	14	9
5	7	15	8
6	6	16	6
7	6	17	8
8	7	18	10
9	11	19	10
10	7	20	8

8. Estimate the number of total chips in the bag. Explain your answer.

9. Copy and complete each statement with the most appropriate fraction: $\frac{1}{4}$, $\frac{1}{6}$, or $\frac{1}{2}$.

More than ▓ of the cookies have at least 8 chips.

More than ▓ of the cookies have at least 9 chips.

More than ▓ of the cookies have at least 10 chips.

10. **a.** A baker makes raisin muffins in batches of four dozen muffins. She pours a box of raisins into each batch. How could you use a sample of muffins to estimate the number of raisins in a box?

b. Suppose there are 1,000 raisins in each box. How many raisins would you expect to find in a typical muffin? Explain.

11. Yung-nan wants to estimate the number of beans in a large jar. She takes out 150 beans and marks each with a red dot. She returns the beans to the jar and mixes them with the unmarked beans. She then takes four samples from the jar. The table shows Yung-nan's data.

Bean Samples

Sample	Total Number of Beans	Number of Beans With Red Dots
1	25	3
2	150	23
3	75	15
4	250	25

a. For each sample, find the relative frequency of total beans that are marked with red dots.

b. Which sample has the greatest percent of marked beans? Use this sample to estimate the number of beans in the jar. Be sure to show your work.

c. Which sample has the least percent of marked beans? Use this sample to estimate the number of beans in the jar. Show your work.

d. Diya used the shaded bars below to make an estimate from Sample 3. Explain what the bars show and how they can be used to estimate the number of beans in the whole jar.

Sample 3

Number of beans in sample: 75

15, or 20% marked			

Whole Jar

Number of beans in jar: ?

150, or 20% marked			

e. Use your answers to parts (a)–(d). What is your best guess for the total number of beans in the jar? Explain your reasoning.

12. Salome is a biologist who studies the albatross, a type of bird. She lives on an island in the Pacific Ocean. Two summers ago, Salome's team trapped 20 albatrosses. They tagged and released them. This past summer, Salome's team trapped 50 albatrosses. They found that two of the albatrosses were tagged.

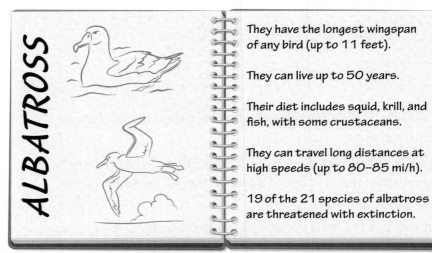

ALBATROSS

They have the longest wingspan of any bird (up to 11 feet).

They can live up to 50 years.

Their diet includes squid, krill, and fish, with some crustaceans.

They can travel long distances at high speeds (up to 80–85 mi/h).

19 of the 21 species of albatross are threatened with extinction.

a. Use Salome's findings. Estimate the number of albatrosses on the island. Explain how you made your estimate.

b. How confident are you that your estimate is accurate? Explain your answer.

c. Describe how Salome's team might use the capture–tag–recapture method to track how much the albatross population changes over time.

13. After independently testing many samples, an electric company determines that approximately 2 of every 1,000 light bulbs on the market are defective. Suppose Americans buy over one billion light bulbs each year. Estimate how many of these bulbs are defective.

14. **Multiple Choice** After testing many samples, a milk shipper determines that approximately 3 in every 100 milk cartons leak. The company ships 200,000 cartons of milk every week. About how many of these cartons leak?

    A. 3   **B.** 600   **C.** 2,000   **D.** 6,000

Connections

Graphs tell stories. Suppose you are a news reporter. For Exercises 15 and 16, use the graphs to write a short news paragraph that tells the story portrayed.

15.

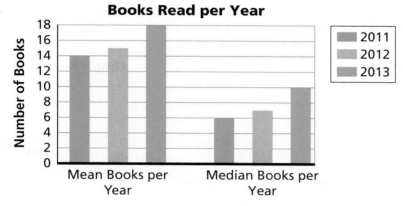

Books Read per Year

Legend: 2011, 2012, 2013

Y-axis: Number of Books (0–18)
X-axis: Mean Books per Year, Median Books per Year

16.

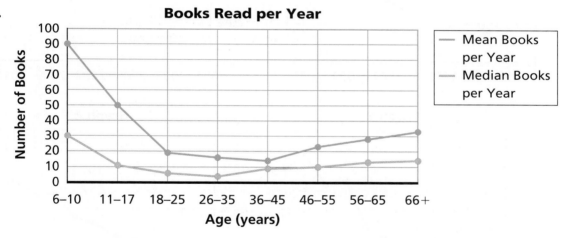

Books Read per Year

Legend: Mean Books per Year, Median Books per Year

Y-axis: Number of Books (0–100)
X-axis: Age (years) — 6–10, 11–17, 18–25, 26–35, 36–45, 46–55, 56–65, 66+

17. Multiple Choice The circle graph shows data for 1,585 students. About how many students are represented by the purple sector?

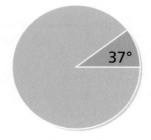

37°

F. 40   **G.** 160   **H.** 590   **J.** 58,650

18. Sometimes graphs can be misleading. The graphs below all display the same data about the percent of paper and paperboard recovered from 2001 to 2012.

   a. Which graph do you think gives the clearest picture of the data pattern? Explain your reasoning.

   b. Why are the other graphs misleading?

Percent of Recovered Paper and Paperboard (2001–2012)

Graph W

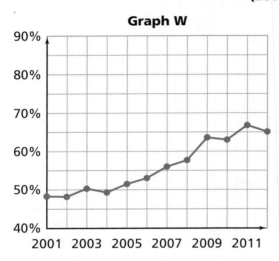

Graph X

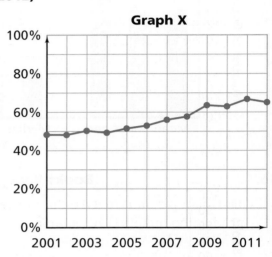

Graph Y

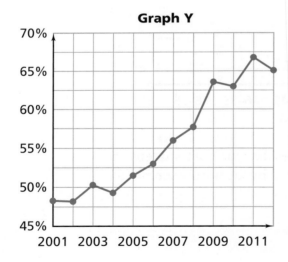

Graph Z

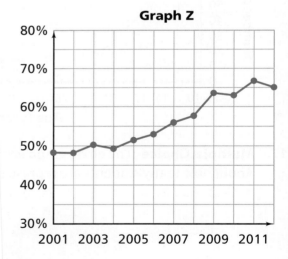

For Exercises 19–23, evaluate each survey described. Use the questions below to help you with your evaluation.

- **What is the goal of the survey?**
- **What population is being studied?**
- **How is the sample chosen?**
- **How are the data analyzed and reported?**
- **Does the analysis support the conclusions?**

19. A television manufacturer wants to design a remote control. Representatives for the company call 1,000 homes with televisions. They find that remote-control users sit an average of 3 meters from their televisions. Based on this finding, the company designs the remote control to work well at distances of 2.5 meters to 3.5 meters from a television.

20. A light bulb manufacturer wants to know the "defect rate" for its product. The manager takes 10 boxes of light bulbs from the assembly line and tests them. Each box contains 50 light bulbs. The manager finds that 5 bulbs are defective. He concludes that production quality is acceptable.

21. A nutritionist wants to know how many Calories in a typical U.S. teenager's diet are from fat. She asks Health teachers in Dallas, Texas to have their students record what they eat during one day. The nutritionist analyzes the records. The median intake is 500 Calories from fat per day, which is the recommended daily allowance. She concludes that Calories from fat are not a problem in the diets of teenagers.

22. A cookie maker claims that there are over 1,000 chocolate chips in a bag of its cookies. A consumer calls the company and asks how it knows this. A spokesperson says the company chooses a sample of bags of cookies. It soaks each bag in cold water to remove everything but the chips. Then the company weighs the chips that remain. In each case, the chips weigh more than a bag of 1,000 chocolate chips.

23. In the cafeteria line, Sam wrinkles his nose when he sees salami subs. The cook asks what he would prefer. Sam replies, "I like bologna better." The cook surveys the next ten students. Seven students say they prefer bologna over salami. The cook decides to serve bologna subs instead of salami subs in the future.

For Exercises 24–28, use the box plot below. Tell whether each statement is *true* or *false*. Explain.

Social Studies Test Scores

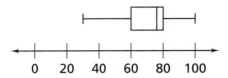

24. The class median is less than 80.

25. Half the class scored between 60 and 80.

26. At least one student earned a score of 100.

27. The class mean is probably less than the median.

28. If there are 30 students in the class, at least 10 scored above 80.

Extensions

29. Use a simulation to help you answer this question:

    If you select five students at random from your class, what is the probability that at least two will have the same birth month?

    a. Design a simulation to model this situation. Tell which month each simulation outcome represents.

    b. Use your birth-month simulation to generate at least 25 samples of five people each. Use your results to estimate the probability that at least two people in a group of five will have the same birth month.

    c. Explain how you could revise your simulation to explore this question:

    What are the chances that at least two students in a class of 25 have the same birthday?

30. The percents of pushpin colors a company produces are on the bulletin board. A school secretary opens a large bag of pushpins. She puts the pins into boxes to distribute to teachers. She puts 50 pins in each box.

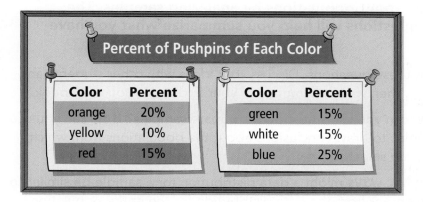

Percent of Pushpins of Each Color

Color	Percent
orange	20%
yellow	10%
red	15%

Color	Percent
green	15%
white	15%
blue	25%

a. How many pushpins of each color would you expect to be in a teacher's box?

b. How might the number of pushpins of each color vary across the boxes?

c. You can simulate filling the boxes by generating random integers from 1 to 20. Which numbers would you use to represent each color? How many numbers do you need to generate at random to simulate filling one box?

d. Carry out the simulation described in part (c) three times. Compare the distributions of colors in your simulated samples with the expected distribution from part (a).

e. Suppose the secretary selects a random sample of 1,000 pushpins from the bag. How closely would you expect the percents of each color in her sample to match the percents in the table?

In this Investigation, you developed strategies to draw conclusions about populations by analyzing samples. The following questions will help you summarize what you have learned.

Think about these questions. Discuss your ideas with other students and your teacher. Then write a summary of your findings in your notebook.

1. **a. How** can you use statistics to compare samples? **How** can you use samples to draw conclusions about the populations from which they are selected?

   b. In what ways might a data distribution for a sample be similar to or different from the data distribution for the entire population?

2. **a. How** can you use box plots, medians, and IQRs to compare samples? Give an example.

   b. How can you use means and MADs to compare samples? Give an example.

   c. How can you use statistics to decide whether differences between samples are expected due to natural variability or reflect measurable differences in underlying populations?

3. **a. How** can you use simulations to generate samples?

   b. How can you use data from a capture–tag–recapture simulation to estimate the actual size of a population?

4. The process of statistical investigation involves posing questions, collecting and analyzing data, and making interpretations to answer the original questions. Choose a Problem from this Investigation. **Explain** how you used the process of statistical investigation to solve the Problem.

Common Core Mathematical Practices

As you worked on the Problems in this Investigation, you used prior knowledge to make sense of them. You also applied Mathematical Practices to solve the Problems. Think back over your work, the ways you thought about the Problems, and how you used Mathematical Practices.

Shawna described her thoughts in the following way:

> In Problem 3.1, I compared arrowhead lengths. I used the mean, median, range, and MAD for each site.
>
> The mean arrowhead length for Site I (39.6 mm) is greater than the mean length for Site II (23.6 mm). The mean length for Site I is between the means for Laddie Creek/Dead Indian Creek (35 mm) and Kobold/Buffalo Creek (45.8 mm). These relationships are similar for the median values, too. Site I was probably settled between 4000 B.C. and A.D. 500.
>
> The data for Site II (mean of 23.6 mm, median of 24 mm) is similar to the Big Goose Creek (mean of 25.3 mm, median of 25.5 mm) and Wortham Shelter data (mean of 26.3 mm, median of 26 mm). Site II must have been settled between A.D. 500 and A.D. 1600.
>
> The minimum data values, maximum data values, and IQRs of all the sites also supported my ideas.

Common Core Standards for Mathematical Practice

MP2 Reason abstractly and quantitatively.

- What other Mathematical Practices can you identify in Shawna's reasoning?

- Describe a Mathematical Practice that you and your classmates used to solve a different Problem in this Investigation.

In this Unit, you learned about sampling data. You used samples to draw conclusions about the populations from which they were taken. You learned how to:

- Analyze and compare sets of data by using measures of center and measures of spread

- Select representative samples by using random sampling techniques

- Collect, organize, and display sample data

- Use your analyses of the samples to draw conclusions about populations

Use Your Understanding of Statistical Reasoning

1. Scientists often study the health of a habitat by gathering data about the number of animals that live there. Suppose you use the capture–tag–recapture method to find out how many butterflies live in a particular field.

   a. Suppose you capture and mark 20 butterflies and then release them. You return to the field and catch 10 butterflies. Only one butterfly is marked. Estimate the size of the population of butterflies in the field. Explain your reasoning.

   b. Suppose you return to the same field on a different day and catch 10 butterflies. Nine butterflies are marked. With this new information, estimate the size of the population of butterflies in the field. Explain.

   c. Suppose you return to the same field on a different day and capture and mark 80 additional butterflies. You then release them. You return to the field and catch 50 butterflies. Twenty-five are marked. Estimate the size of the population of butterflies in the field.

   d. For each part (a)–(c), how might you change your estimate to make sure that it is close to the actual number of butterflies in the field?

2. Glove makers are interested in the lengths and widths of their customers' hands. They look for patterns so they can make gloves that will fit most people. Each data value in the dot plots on the next page represents the mean of a sample of hand lengths.

- Two dot plots display data collected from 100 samples of males.

- Two dot plots display data collected from 100 samples of females.

- Two dot plots (one male and one female) show data from 100 samples of size 10.

- Two dot plots (one male and one female) show data from 100 samples of size 30.

- Assume that, on average, men's hands are longer than women's.

a. Which two distributions show data collected from males? Which two distributions show data collected from females? Explain your reasoning.

b. Look at the distributions of male data. Which distribution shows means from 100 samples of 10 males each? From 100 samples of 30 males each? Justify your reasoning.

c. Look at the distributions of female data. Which distribution shows means from 100 samples of 10 females each? From 100 samples of 30 females each? Justify your reasoning.

d. Compare the distribution of data collected from 100 samples of 30 males each with the distribution of data collected from 100 samples of 30 females each. How are the distributions alike? How are they different?

e. The MAD for the distribution of data collected from 100 samples of 30 males each is 0.072 centimeter. The MAD for the distribution of data collected from 100 samples of 30 females each is 0.077 centimeter.

How can you use this new information to support your answer to part (d)? What other comparisons can you now make?

Figure A

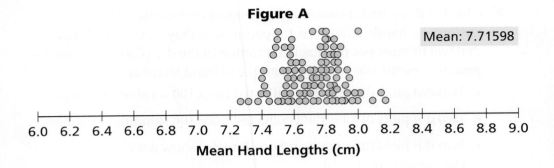

Mean: 7.71598

Mean Hand Lengths (cm)

Figure B

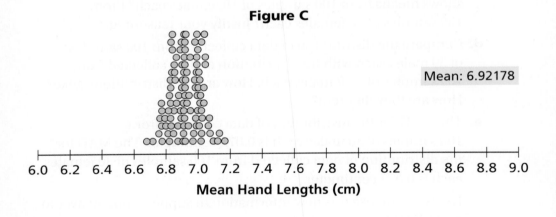

Mean: 6.90999

Mean Hand Lengths (cm)

Figure C

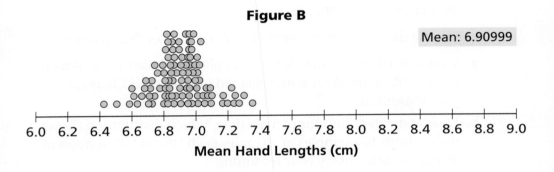

Mean: 6.92178

Mean Hand Lengths (cm)

Figure D

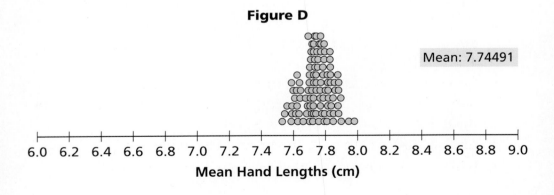

Mean: 7.74491

Mean Hand Lengths (cm)

3. Below are two box plots. One box plot is constructed from the data collected from 100 samples of 30 males each from Exercise 2. The other is constructed from the data collected from 100 samples of 30 females each from Exercise 2.

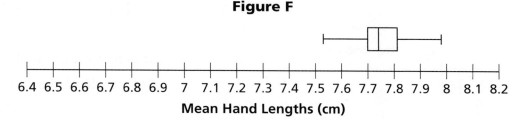

Figure E

6.4 6.5 6.6 6.7 6.8 6.9 7 7.1 7.2 7.3 7.4 7.5 7.6 7.7 7.8 7.9 8 8.1 8.2
Mean Hand Lengths (cm)

Figure F

6.4 6.5 6.6 6.7 6.8 6.9 7 7.1 7.2 7.3 7.4 7.5 7.6 7.7 7.8 7.9 8 8.1 8.2
Mean Hand Lengths (cm)

a. Which box plot shows data for males? For females? Explain.

b. Identify the IQR from each box plot. Do these IQRs support your answers for Exercise 2, parts (d) and (e)? Explain.

c. What other comparisons can you make using the box plots?

Explain Your Reasoning

When you choose samples, compare data sets, and use statistics to draw conclusions about populations, you should be able to justify your reasoning.

4. When you report the mean, what related measure of spread can you report? What does this measure tell you about the data distribution?

5. When you report the median, what related measure of spread can you report? What does this measure tell you about the data distribution?

6. Describe three kinds of sampling methods that are not random sampling. Identify each method's strengths and weaknesses. Give an example of each kind of method.

7. Give an example of a random sampling technique.

8. When should you use sampled data to study a population?

English / Spanish Glossary

B **bar graph** A graphical representation of a table of data in which the height or length of each bar indicates its frequency. The bars are separated from each other to highlight that the data are discrete or "counted" data. In a vertical bar graph, the horizontal axis shows the values or categories, and the vertical axis shows the frequency for each of the values or categories. In a horizontal bar graph, the vertical axis shows the values or categories, and the horizontal axis shows the frequencies.

gráfica de barras Representación gráfica de una tabla de datos en la que la altura o la longitud de cada barra indica su frecuencia. Las barras están separadas entre sí para subrayar que los datos son discretos o "contados". En una gráfica de barras vertical, el eje horizontal representa los valores o categorías y el eje vertical representa la frecuencia de cada uno de los valores o categorías. En una gráfica de barras horizontal, el eje vertical representa los valores o categorías y el eje horizontal representa las frecuencias.

Vertical Bar Graph

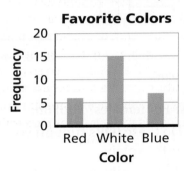

Horizontal Bar Graph

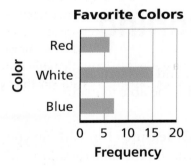

Gráfica de barras vertical

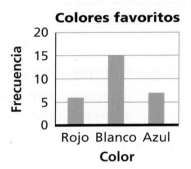

Gráfica de barras horizontal

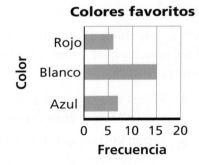

box-and-whisker plot, or box plot A display that shows the distribution of values in a data set separated into four equal-size groups. A box plot is constructed from a five-number summary of the data.

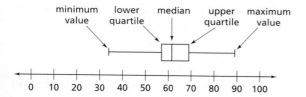

gráfica de caja y bigotes o diagrama de caja Una representación que muestra la distribución de los valores de un conjunto de datos separados en cuatro grupos de igual tamaño. Un diagrama de caja se construye a partir de un resumen de cinco números de los datos.

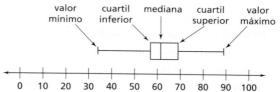

capture–tag–recapture method A sampling method used to estimate the size of a wildlife population. When using this method, scientists take a sample of animals, mark them in some way, then release them back into their habitat. Later, they capture another sample and count how many animals in that sample are marked. They use these data to estimate the population size.

método de captura-marcaje y recaptura Un método de muestreo que se usa para estimar el tamaño de una población de animales silvestres. Al usar este método, los científicos toman una muestra de los animales, los marcan de alguna manera y luego los vuelven a liberar en su hábitat. Más tarde, capturan otra muestra y cuentan cuántos animales de esa muestra están marcados. Usan estos datos para estimar el tamaño de la población.

categorical data Non-numerical data sets are categorical. For example, the responses to "What month were you born?" are categorical data. Frequency counts can be made of the values for a given category. The table below shows examples of categories and their possible values.

datos categóricos Los conjuntos de datos no numéricos son categóricos. Por ejemplo, las respuestas a "¿En qué mes naciste?" son datos categóricos. Los conteos de frecuencia se pueden hacer a partir de los valores de una categoría dada. La siguiente tabla muestra ejemplos de categorías y sus posibles valores.

Category	Possible Values
Month people are born	January, February, March
Favorite color to wear	magenta, blue, yellow
Kinds of pets people have	cats, dogs, fish, horses

Categoría	Valores posibles
Mes de nacimiento de las personas	enero, febrero, marzo
Color preferido para vestir	magenta, azul, amarillo
Tipos de mascotas que tienen las personas	gatos, perros, peces, caballos

census Data collected from every individual in a population.

censo Los datos recopilados de todos los individuos de una población.

English/Spanish Glossary

convenience sampling Choosing a sample because it is convenient. For example, if you ask all the students on your bus how long it takes them to get to school and then claim that these data are representative of the entire school population, you are surveying a convenience sample.

muestreo de conveniencia Una muestra seleccionada porque es conveniente. Por ejemplo, si les preguntas a todos los estudiantes que van en el autobús cuánto tiempo tardan en llegar a la escuela y luego afirmas que esos datos son representativos de toda la población escolar, estás aplicando un muestreo de conveniencia.

D **describe** Academic Vocabulary
To explain or tell in detail. A written description can contain facts and other information needed to communicate your answer. A diagram or a graph may also be included.

related terms *express, explain, illustrate*

sample The band members want to conduct a survey. Describe a plan that uses systematic sampling.

describir Vocabulario académico
Explicar o decir con detalle. Una descripción escrita puede contener datos y otro tipo de información necesaria para comunicar tu respuesta. También puede incluir un diagrama o una gráfica.

términos relacionados *expresar, explicar, ilustrar*

ejemplo Los integrantes de la banda quieren hacer una encuesta. Describe un plan que use el muestreo sistemático.

> The band members can randomly select a starting time and then survey every sixth student who enters the school. This gives the band members a methodical way of collecting data.

> Los integrantes de la banda pueden seleccionar al azar un tiempo de inicio y luego aplicar la encuesta a cada sexto estudiante que entre a la escuela. Esto da a los integrantes de la banda una manera metódica de recopilar datos.

distribution The entire set of collected data values, organized to show their frequency of occurrence. A distribution can be described using summary statistics and/or by referring to its shape.

distribución Todo el conjunto de valores de datos recopilados, organizados para mostrar su frecuencia de incidencia. Una distribución se puede describir usando la estadística sumaria y/o haciendo referencia a su forma.

....

estimate Academic Vocabulary
To find an approximate answer that is relatively close to an exact amount.

related terms *approximate, guess*

sample A cup manufacturer knows that approximately 4 out of every 2,000 cups are defective. Estimate how many of 10,000 cups bought by a restaurant will be defective.

hacer una estimación Vocabulario académico
Hallar una respuesta aproximada que esté relativamente cerca de una cantidad exacta.

términos relacionados *aproximar, suponer*

ejemplo Un fabricante de tazas sabe que aproximadamente 4 de cada 2,000 tazas son defectuosas. Estima cuántas de 10,000 tazas compradas por un restaurante son defectuosas.

I can write 4 out of 2,000 as a percent.
$$\frac{4}{2,000} = 0.002 = 0.2\%$$
Then I can multiply 10,000 by 0.2% to estimate the number of defective cups bought by the restaurant chain.
$$0.002 \times 10,000 = 20$$
About 20 of the cups are defective.
I can also use a proportion.
$$\frac{4}{2,000} = \frac{x}{10,000}$$
$$2,000x = 40,000$$
$$x = 20$$

Puedo escribir 4 de 2,000 como un porcentaje. $\frac{4}{2,000} = 0.002 = 0.2\%$
Luego, puedo multiplicar 10,000 por 0.2% para estimar el número de tazas defectuosas compradas por el restaurante.
$$0.002 \times 10,000 = 20$$
Alrededor de 20 de las tazas están defectuosas.
También puedo usar una proporción.
$$\frac{4}{2,000} = \frac{x}{10,000}$$
$$2,000x = 40,000$$
$$x = 20$$

expect Academic Vocabulary
To use theoretical or experimental data to anticipate a certain outcome.

related terms *anticipate, predict*

sample A cook makes trail mix in 2-pound batches. She puts a bag of almonds into each batch. There are about 120 almonds in each bag. Explain how many almonds you would expect to find in $\frac{1}{2}$ pound of trail mix.

> If I divide 2 pounds of trail mix into half-pound parts, I will have 4 parts. Since the cook puts 120 almonds into each batch, divide 120 by 4 to determine the expected number of almonds in one-half pound. I can expect to find 30 almonds in one-half pound of trail mix because 120 ÷ 4 = 30.

esperar Vocabulario académico
Usar datos teóricos o experimentales para anticipar un resultado determinado.

términos relacionados *anticipar, predecir*

ejemplo Una cocinera prepara una mezcla de nueces y frutas secas en recetas de 2 libras. Pone una bolsa de almendras en cada receta. Hay aproximadamente 120 almendras en cada bolsa. Explica cuántas almendras esperarías hallar en media libra de mezcla de nueces y frutas secas.

> Si divido 2 libras de mezcla de nueces y frutas secas en partes de media libra, tendré 4 partes. Dado que la cocinera pone 120 almendras en cada receta, divido 120 por 4 para determinar el número esperado de almendras en media libra. Puedo esperar hallar 30 almendras en media libra de mezcla de nueces y frutas secas, porque 120 ÷ 4 = 30.

explain Academic Vocabulary

To give facts and details that make an idea easier to understand. Explaining can involve a written summary supported by a diagram, chart, table, or a combination of these.

related terms *analyze, clarify, describe, justify, tell*

sample Explain why the line graph is misleading.

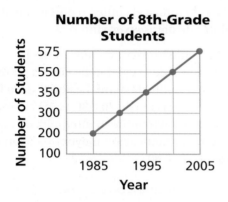

The vertical axis of the graph does not start with zero and does not increase by the same amount for each interval. This causes the data to appear to increase at a constant rate, but it is increasing at different rates. Therefore, the graph is misleading.

explicar Vocabulario académico

Dar datos y detalles que hacen que una idea sea más fácil de comprender. Explicar puede incluir un resumen escrito apoyado por un diagrama, una gráfica, una tabla o una combinación de estos.

términos relacionados *analizar, aclarar, describir, justificar, decir*

ejemplo Explica por qué la gráfica lineal es engañosa.

El eje vertical de la gráfica no empieza en cero y no aumenta en la misma cantidad en cada intervalo. Esto hace que los datos parezcan aumentar en una tasa constante, pero están aumentando en diferentes tasas. Por tanto, la gráfica es engañosa.

---

five-number summary The minimum value, lower quartile, median, upper quartile, and maximum value for a data set. These five values give a summary of the shape of the distribution and are used to make box plots. The five-number summary is noted on the box plot below.

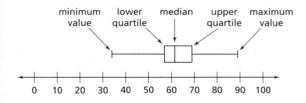

resumen de cinco números El valor mínimo, el cuartil inferior, la mediana, el cuartil superior y el valor máximo de un conjunto de datos. Estos cinco valores dan un resumen de la forma de una distribución y se usan para construir diagramas de caja. El resumen de cinco números se observa en el siguiente diagrama de caja.

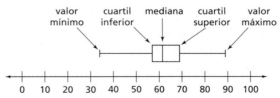

frequency The number of times a given data value occurs in a data set.

frecuencia El número de veces que un valor de datos dado se produce en un conjunto de datos.

H **histogram** A display that shows the distribution of numeric data. The range of data values, divided into intervals, is displayed on the horizontal axis. The vertical axis shows the frequency in numbers or in percents. The height of the bar over each interval indicates the count or percent of data values in that interval.

histograma Una representación que muestra la distribución de datos numéricos. El rango de valores de datos, dividido en intervalos, se representa en el eje horizontal. El eje vertical muestra la frecuencia en números o en porcentajes. La altura de la barra sobre cada intervalo indica el conteo o porcentaje de valores de datos en ese intervalo.

The histogram below shows quality ratings for certain brands of peanut butter. The height of the bar over the interval from 20 to 30 is 4. This indicates that four brands of peanut butter have quality ratings greater than or equal to 20 and less than 30.

El siguiente histograma representa la calificación de la calidad de ciertas marcas de mantequilla de maní. La altura de la barra sobre el intervalo de 20 a 30 es 4. Esto indica que cuatro marcas de mantequilla de maní tienen una calificación mayor que o igual a 20 y menor que 30.

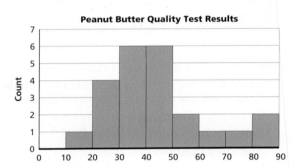

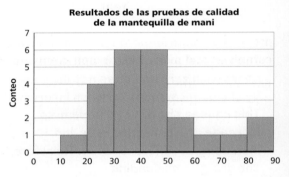

I **interquartile range (IQR)** The difference of the values of the upper quartile (Q3) and the lower quartile (Q1). In the box-and-whisker plot below, the upper quartile is 69, and the lower quartile is 58. The IQR is the difference 69–58, or 11.

rango entre cuartiles (REC) La diferencia de los valores del cuartil superior (C3) y el cuartil inferior (C1). En el siguiente diagrama de caja y bigotes, el cuartil superior es 69 y el cuartil inferior es 58. El REC es la diferencia de 69 a 58, u 11.

$$IQR = 69 - 58 = 11$$

$$REC = 69 - 58 = 11$$

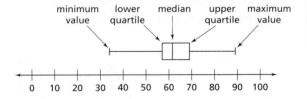

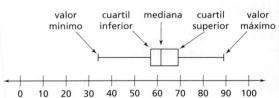

line plot A way to organize data along a number line where the ✗s (or other symbols) above a number represent how often each value occurs in a data set. A line plot made with dots is sometimes referred to as a dot plot.

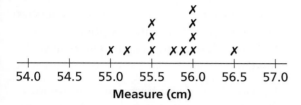

Measure (cm)

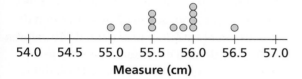

Measure (cm)

diagrama de puntos Una manera de organizar los datos a lo largo de una recta numérica donde las ✗ (u otros símbolos) colocadas encima de un número representan la frecuencia con que se menciona cada valor. Un diagrama de puntos hecho con puntos algunas veces se conoce como gráfica de puntos.

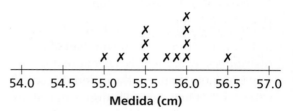

Medida (cm)

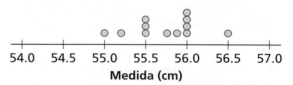

Medida (cm)

- -

mean The value found when all the data are combined and then redistributed evenly.

For example, the total number of siblings for the data in the line plot below is 56. If all 19 students had the same number of siblings, they would each have about 3 siblings.

Differences from the mean "balance out" so that the sum of differences below and above the mean equal 0. The mean of a set of data is the sum of the values divided by the number of values in the set.

Number of Siblings Students Have

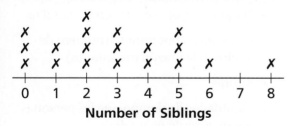

Number of Siblings

media El valor que se halla cuando todos los datos se combinan y luego se redistribuyen de manera uniforme.

Por ejemplo, el número total de hermanos y hermanas en los datos del siguiente diagrama es 56. Si los 19 estudiantes tuvieran la misma cantidad de hermanos y hermanas, cada uno tendría aproximadamente 3 hermanos o hermanas.

Las diferencias de la media se "equilibran" de manera que la suma de las diferencias por encima y por debajo de la media sea igual a 0. La media de un conjunto de datos es la suma de los valores dividida por el número de valores en el conjunto.

Número de hermanos y hermanas que tienen los estudiantes

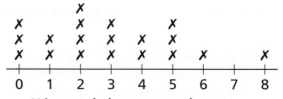

Número de hermanos y hermanas

mean absolute deviation (MAD) The average distance of all of the data values in a data set from the mean of the distribution.

median The number that marks the midpoint of an ordered set of data. At least half of the values lie at or above the median, and at least half lie at or below the median.

For the sibling data (0, 0, 0, 1, 1, 2, 2, 2, 2, 3, 3, 3, 4, 4, 5, 5, 5, 6, 8), the median of the distribution of siblings is 3 because the tenth (middle) value in the ordered set of 19 values is 3. When a distribution contains an even number of data values, the median is computed by finding the average of the two middle data values in an ordered list of the data values.

For example, the median of 1, 3, 7, 8, 25, and 30 is 7.5 because the data values 7 and 8 are third and fourth in the list of six data values.

mode The value that appears most frequently in a set of data. In the data set 2, 2, 2, 2, 3, 3, 7, 7, 8, 9, 10, 11, the mode is 2.

numerical data Values that are numbers such as counts, measurements, and ratings. Here are some examples.

- Number of children in families
- Pulse rates (number of heart beats per minute)
- Heights
- Amounts of time people spend reading in one day
- Ratings such as: on a scale of 1 to 5 with 1 as "low interest," how would you rate your interest in participating in the school's field day?

desviación absoluta media (DAM) La distancia media de todos los valores de datos en un conjunto de datos a partir de la media de la distribución.

mediana El número que marca el punto medio de un conjunto ordenado de datos. Por lo menos la mitad de los datos se encuentran en o encima de la mediana y por lo menos la mitad se encuentran en o debajo de la mediana.

Para los datos de los hermanos y hermanas (0, 0, 0, 1, 1, 2, 2, 2, 2, 3, 3, 3, 4, 4, 5, 5, 5, 6, 8), la mediana de la distribución de hermanos y hermanas es 3 porque el décimo valor (el del medio) en el conjunto ordenado de 19 valores es 3. Cuando una distribución contiene un número par de valores de datos, la mediana se calcula hallando el promedio de los dos valores de datos del medio en una lista ordenada de los valores de datos.

Por ejemplo, la mediana de 1, 3, 7, 8, 25 y 30 es 7.5, porque los valores de datos 7 y 8 son tercero y cuarto en la lista de seis valores de datos.

moda El valor que aparece con mayor frecuencia en un conjunto de datos. En el conjunto de datos 2, 2, 2, 2, 3, 3, 7, 7, 8, 9, 10, 11, la moda es 2.

datos numéricos Valores que son números como conteos, mediciones y calificaciones. Los siguientes son algunos ejemplos.

- Número de hijos e hijas en las familias
- Pulsaciones por minuto (número de latidos del corazón por minuto)
- Alturas
- Cantidades de tiempo que las personas pasan leyendo en un día
- Calificaciones como: en una escala de 1 a 5, en la que 1 representa "poco interés", ¿cómo calificarías tu interés por participar en el día de maniobras de tu escuela?

outlier A value that lies far from the "center" of a distribution and is not like other values. *Outlier* is a relative term, but it indicates a data point that is much higher or much lower than the values that could be normally expected for the distribution.

To identify an outlier in a distribution represented by a box plot, measure the distance between Q3 and any suspected outliers at the top of the range of data values; if this distance is more than $1.5 \times$ IQR, then the data value is an outlier. Likewise, if the distance between any data value at the low end of the range of values and Q1 is more than $1.5 \times$ IQR, then the data value is an outlier.

valor extremo Un valor que se encuentra lejos del "centro" de una distribución y no es como los demás valores. El *valor extremo* es un término relativo, pero indica un dato que es mucho más alto o mucho más bajo que los valores que se podrían esperar normalmente para la distribución.

Para identificar un valor extremo en una distribución representada por un diagrama de caja, se mide la distancia entre C3 y cualquier valor que se sospeche es extremo en la parte superior del rango de los valores de datos; si esta distancia es mayor que $1.5 \times$ REC, entonces el valor de datos es un valor extremo. Del mismo modo, si la distancia entre cualquier valor de datos en la parte inferior del rango de valores y C1 es mayor que $1.5 \times$ REC, entonces el valor de datos es un valor extremo.

population The entire collection of people or objects you are studying.

población El grupo completo de las personas o los objetos que se están estudiando.

quartile One of three points that divide a data set into four equal groups. The second quartile, Q2, is the median of the data set. The first quartile, Q1, is the median of the lower half of the data set. The third quartile, Q3, is the median of the upper half of the data set.

cuartil Uno de los tres puntos que dividen un conjunto de datos en cuatro grupos iguales. El segundo cuartil, C2, es la mediana del conjunto de datos. El primer cuartil, C1, es la mediana de la mitad inferior del conjunto de datos. El tercer cuartil, C3, es la mediana de la mitad superior del conjunto de datos.

random sampling Choosing a sample in a way that gives every member of a population an equally likely chance of being selected.

muestreo aleatorio Elegir una muestra de manera que todo miembro de una población tenga la misma probabilidad de ser seleccionado.

range The difference of the maximum value and the minimum value in a distribution. If you know the range of the data is 12 grams of sugar per serving, you know that the difference between the minimum and maximum values is 12 grams. For example, in the distribution 2, 2, 2, 2, 3, 3, 7, 7, 8, 9, 10, 11, the range of the data set is 9, because $11 - 2 = 9$.

rango La diferencia del valor máximo y el valor mínimo en una distribución. Si se sabe que el rango de los datos es 12 gramos de azúcar por porción, entonces se sabe que la diferencia entre el valor mínimo y el máximo es 12 gramos. Por ejemplo, en la distribución 2, 2, 2, 2, 3, 3, 7, 7, 8, 9, 10, 11, el rango del conjunto de datos es 9, porque $11 - 2 = 9$.

relative frequency The ratio of the number of desired results to the total number of trials. Written as a percent, relative frequencies help you compare samples of different sizes.

frecuencia relativa La razón del número de resultados deseados al número total de pruebas. Escritas como porcentajes, las frecuencias relativas ayudan a comparar muestras de diferentes tamaños.

representative sample A sample whose characteristics accurately reflect those of the larger population from which the sample was selected.

muestra representativa Una muestra cuyas características reflejan con exactitud las características de la población más grande de la que se seleccionó la muestra.

S **sample** A group of people or objects selected from a population.

muestra Un grupo de personas u objetos seleccionados de una población.

sampling distribution The distribution of the means (or medians) from a set of same-size samples, each selected randomly from the same population.

distribución muestral Distribución de las medias (o medianas) de un conjunto de muestras del mismo tamaño, seleccionadas al azar de la misma población.

sampling plan A detailed strategy for selecting a sample from a population, including what data will be collected, in what manner, and by whom.

plan de muestreo Una estrategia detallada para seleccionar la muestra de una población, incluyendo los datos que se recopilarán, de qué manera y por quién.

simulate To run an experiment modeling the relevant characteristics of a real-world situation for use in studying the behavior of the real-world situation.

simular Llevar a cabo un experimento representando las características relevantes de una situación de la vida diaria para usarlas en el estudio del comportamiento de esa situación.

systematic sampling Choosing a sample in a methodical way. For example, if you survey every tenth person on an alphabetical list of names, you are surveying a systematic sample.

muestreo sistemático Una muestra seleccionada de una manera metódica. Por ejemplo, si se encuesta a cada décima persona de una lista de nombres en orden alfabético, se estaría aplicando el muestreo sistemático.

V **voluntary-response (or self-selected) sampling** A sample that selects itself. For example, if you put an ad in the school paper asking for volunteers to take a survey, the students who respond will be a voluntary-response sample.

muestra de respuesta voluntaria (o autoseleccionada) Una muestra que se selecciona a sí misma. Por ejemplo, si se pone un anuncio en el periódico escolar pidiendo voluntarios para participar en una encuesta, los estudiantes que respondan serán una muestra de respuesta voluntaria.

Index

Acknowledgments

Cover Design

Three Communication Design, Chicago

Text

American Forest and Paper Association

076 Data from the **"Paper & Paperboard Recovery"** from
WWW.PAPERRECYCLES.ORG

George C. Knight

057 From **"Site 1 and Site 2 Arrowhead Sizes"** by George C. Knight and James
D. Keyser from PLAINS ANTHROPOLOGIST VOLUME 28, NUMBER 101, 1983.
Reprinted by permission of the author.

058 From **"A Mathematical Technique for Dating Projectile Points Common to
the Northwestern Plains (Big Goose Creek Arrowheads)"** by George C. Knight
and James D. Keyser from PLAINS ANTHROPOLOGIST VOLUME 28,
NUMBER 101, 1983. Reprinted by permission of the author.

058 From **"A Mathematical Technique for Dating Projectile Points Common to
the Northwestern Plains (Wortham Shelter Arrowheads)"** by George C. Knight
and James D. Keyser from PLAINS ANTHROPOLOGIST VOLUME 28,
NUMBER 101, 1983. Reprinted by permission of the author.

059 From **"A Mathematical Technique for Dating Projectile Points Common
to the Northwestern Plains (Kobold/Buffalo Creek Arrowheads)"** by George
C. Knight and James D. Keyser from PLAINS ANTHROPOLOGIST VOLUME 28,
NUMBER 101, 1983. Reprinted by permission of the author.

059 From **"A Mathematical Technique for Dating Projectile Points Common
to the Northwestern Plains (Laddie Creek/Dead Indian Creek Arrowheads)"**
by George C. Knight and James D. Keyser from PLAINS ANTHROPOLOGIST
VOLUME 28, NUMBER 101, 1983. Reprinted by permission of the author.

Duane Marden

016 "Roller Coaster Census Report" by Duane Marden from
WWW.RCDB.COM/CENSUS.HTM

National Geographic Stock

026 "Survey 2000: Census Information" from
WWW.NATIONALGEOGRAPHIC.COM. Used by permission of NGS/National
Geographic Stock.

Pew Research Center

034 Data on teen text messaging and teen cell phone ownership from the Pew
Research Center from WWW.PEWRESEARCH.ORG

Photographs

Photo locators denoted as follows: Top (T), Center (C), Bottom (B), Left (L), Right (R), Background (Bkgd)

002 (TR) AndreAnita/Shutterstock , (BR) David R. Frazier Photolibrary, Inc./Alamy; **003** Fritz Polking/The Image Works; **070** Hemera Technologies/Alamy; **074** AndreAnita/Shutterstock; **016** (BL) David R. Frazier Photolibrary, Inc./Alamy, (BR) David Kleyn/Alamy; **034** (BL) iStockphoto/Thinkstock, (BCL) Milosluz/Fotolia, (BCR) Marco Desscouleurs/Fotolia, (CR) SP-PIC/Fotolia; **056** Alberto Paredes/Alamy; **057** Hemera Technologies/Alamy.

Acknowledgments